Brand Power

Brand Power

Edited by

Paul Stobart
Director, Interbrand Group plc

First published 1994 by
MACMILLAN PRESS LTD
Houndmills, Basingstoke, Hampshire RG21 6XS
and London
Companies and representatives
throughout the world

ISBN 0–333–57013–8

A catalogue record for this book is available
from the British Library.

10   9   8   7   6   5   4   3
04   03   02   01   00   99   98   97   96

Printed in Great Britain by
Biddles Ltd
Guildford and King's Lynn

Contents

List of Figures

List of Illustrations

List of Plates

x

Acknowledgements

The editor and publishers would like to thank all those brand owners and their agents and associates who have supplied information and illustrations for this book. It should be mentioned that virtually every product or corporate name mentioned in the book is a registered trade mark and virtually every logo reproduced in the book is the specific property of a company.

Notes on the Contributors

Luciano Benetton is President of Benetton Group SpA, world leader in the design, manufacture and distribution of casual clothing for men, women and children.

Michael Birkin is Group Chief Executive of Interbrand Group plc, the leading branding consultancy, and has considerable experience in the brand valuation field.

Carsten Dahlman is a senior partner of Siar Bossard, the Scandinavian arm of the international management consultancy group, Groupe Bossard.

Dr Bradley Gale is the founder of Market Driven Quality Inc, a market strategy firm based in the USA. He served for 12 years as Research Director for the PIMS* programme (* Profit Impact of Market Strategy).

Donald Keough has recently retired from his position as President and Chief Operating Officer of the Coca-Cola Company, the world's largest manufacturer of soft drinks and owner of one of the world's true power brands, Coca-Cola.

Terry Leahy is Marketing Director of Tesco Group plc, one of Britain's largest and most successful food retailing organisations.

John Murphy is Chairman of Interbrand Group plc, the leading branding consultancy, and an acknowledged expert on brand strategy.

Keijiro Nakabe is President of Maruha Corporation, the biggest food and fishery group in Japan.

The late Professor Werner Niefer was President of Mercedes-Benz AG, the manufacturer of luxury motor cars, buses and trucks. Shortly after his retirement from Mercedes-Benz Professor Niefer died. Professor Niefer presided over Mercedes-Benz at a time of significant growth and expansion. He will be sorely missed by all who knew him.

Camillo Pagano was previously Executive Vice-President of Nestlé SA, responsible for International Brand Development until his retirement in 1992.

Garo Partoyan is General Counsel, Marketing and Technology, for Mars Incorporated, owner of the internationally renowned Mars confectionery brand.

Nicolò Polla is Marketing Director of SpA Egidio Galbani, the world's largest manufacturer of branded cheese. Egidio Galbani is now part of the BSN Group.

Sir Allen Sheppard is Chairman of Grand Metropolitan plc, one of Britain's largest companies and owner of some of the world's most powerful food and drinks brands.

Paul Stobart (editor) is a Director of Interbrand Group plc, the leading branding consultancy.

Sir Anthony Tennant has just retired from his position of Chairman of Guinness plc, owners of the famous Guinness stout and a large portfolio of internationally acclaimed spirits' brands.

Preface

Paul Stobart
Editor

An increasing number of the world's most influential companies have come to recognise that their brands are of enormous value and that failure to maintain and support these important assets can lead to failure of the company itself.

Many in the world of marketing have commented over the years on the power of individual brands and the value that they have in contributing to the financial well-being of a company. Seldom, however, have the *owners* of the world's leading brands been invited to give their views on the importance of brands and branding. With this in mind, my colleagues and I at Interbrand set out to establish whether leading brand owners would be interested in contributing to a book whose primary objective was to provide brand owners with the opportunity to put forward their own views on the power and importance of brands. The response was over-whelming – brand owners from all round the world were keen to take part in what they believed to be an important initiative.

The title of the book, *Brand Power*, was chosen quite deliberately. Brands are powerful strategic weapons which, if handled correctly and managed sensibly, can provide their owners with considerable rewards. If brand power is harnessed effectively, growth in market share and corporate profitability normally follows.

The topics covered in this book are all connected in some way with the central theme of the importance of brand power. Contributions from senior executives from Coca-Cola, Guinness, Nestlé, Grand Metropolitan, Mercedes-Benz, BSN,

Benetton, Tesco and Mars cover subjects such as the importance of brand power and how to create, manage and value brand power. The Japanese perspective on the potential for power branding in the Japanese market is put forward by the President of Maruha Corporation, one of the world's leading fishery and food manufacturing groups. And, although the views of the world's great brand owners form the centrepiece to this book, I have also included important contributions from academics, management consultants and marketing experts.

I would like to thank all the contributors to this book for all the work they have put into their respective chapters. It has been a great privilege to work so closely with such a knowledgeable panel. Without them and their efforts this book would not have been possible.

I am also grateful to many of my colleagues at Interbrand for their support and help during the preparation of *Brand Power*. In particular I would like to thank Debbie Kitson and Claire Yates, who were responsible for much of the administrative control of what proved to be a highly complex and logistically difficult process. I am also indebted to John Murphy, Chairman of Interbrand, whose advice and assistance proved so helpful throughout the entire *Brand Power* project.

London   PAUL STOBART

Introduction

Paul Stobart
Director
INTERBRAND GROUP PLC

Branding has been used since the earliest times to distinguish the goods of one producer from those of another. Indeed, the word 'brand' derives from the Old Norse word *brandr*, which means to burn. Brands were, and still are, the means by which owners of cattle mark their animals as their own. From branding cattle and other livestock, early man moved on to brand all his other chattels – a potter identified his pots by putting his thumbprint into the wet clay at the bottom of the pot or by making some other form of mark such as a star, a cross or a circle. The mark represented proof of origin of the product and was important information to purchasers who wanted to buy that particular potter's products. The potter, by identifying his products in this way, was able to provide his customers with a means of recognising and specifying his products. From the customer's perspective, of course, the presence of marks on pots and other goods provided a means of avoiding those products which the customer did not want to buy.

The practice of branding has developed out of all recognition from these early times but most of this progress has only taken place in the last hundred years. Indeed, it was the advent of the industrial revolution and the improved transportation systems that came with it that provided the real impetus for the development of branding.

Many of today's great brands, among them Coca-Cola and Kodak (see Plate 1), owe their existence to the explosion of

1

economic growth that resulted from the new, fast and efficient communications systems brought about by railways and steam-driven ships. Until these sophisticated transportation systems were introduced, manufacturers found it difficult to distribute their products very widely except by using barges or sailing ships, both of which took a long time. Some trade in branded goods did exist between ports and their immediate hinterlands (cocoa, for example, was transported to Cadbury's factory in Bournville by barge and the finished chocolate product was returned to the port for onward distribution in the same manner) but such distribution systems were limited in scope and quite rare.

The railways changed all this forever. In the USA, farmers in the mid-West were able to get their produce to the Eastern Seaboard or to the West Coast at great speed and at much-reduced cost. Companies that invested in expanding their operations and opening up new markets in different geographic locations became aware of the importance of developing a brand name for their products that people all over the country would recognise. Mr Procter and Mr Gamble's soap-making business in Cincinnati and Mr Kraft's cheese-making business in Chicago both prospered at the expense of less resourceful, less daring and less skilful competitors. Their high quality, branded, differentiated products began to establish themselves as leading products right across the USA.

This process was repeated all over the world. Before the introduction of the railways to the United Kingdom most villages and towns had their own breweries serving the local community with their beer requirements. The advent of the railways meant that beer could be transported great distances and sold to publicans right across the country. The breweries that had the best beer and the most innovative means of promoting and distributing it benefited at the expense of the others. Less efficient local beer producers began to be squeezed out of business. Consumers began to pick and choose which beer they bought with much more circumspection than previously. Nowadays leading beer brands are manufactured and distributed worldwide.

Trade Mark Law

This rapid development of branding and the development of valuable and powerful property rights in brand names has led in turn to profound developments in the area of trade mark law. From earliest times people recognised the importance of protecting their marks from the dangers of counterfeiting. Indeed, the practice of counterfeiting has been in existence as long as man himself. The Belgae, for example, exported large quantities of counterfeit Roman pottery into Britain prior to Julius Caesar's invasion. For hundreds of years Roman products had been available, at a price, to the Ancient Britons and had come to be prized by them for their superior quality and sophistication. The Belgae developed a thriving trade in counterfeit Roman pottery with fake brands – squiggles which their customers thought were Latin. No doubt not all of the customers were fooled but the practice had the effect of enriching the Belgian potters at the expense of the Romans.

Over the centuries comprehensive legal systems have been developed to ensure that trade marks can be protected against counterfeiting. Trade mark laws now exist in virtually every country in the world and confer powerful rights upon trade mark owners wishing to protect and maintain their marks against abuse or infringement.

The first Trade Mark Bill in the United Kingdom was drafted in 1862 and became law in 1875. The first registered trade mark in Britain was the Bass Red Triangle (Plate 2), a mark which is still in widespread use today, nearly 120 years later. The Bass Red Triangle is also one of the elite marks that has successfully crossed the threshold from commerce to art – it figures prominently in Manet's 'Bar at the Folies Bérgère', painted in 1882.

Many brand names which have great power today were first launched over 100 years ago. Coca-Cola was launched in Atlanta, Georgia in 1886. American Express travellers cheques, Quaker Oats (Plate 3), Heinz baked beans, Jaeger underwear and Ivory soap were all leading brands in the 1880s and 1890s and still are today.

Services

The concept of branding has been extended successfully to services, especially over the last thirty to forty years. Indeed some of the greatest successes in marketing in the last few decades have taken place in the services field. Great international brands like Visa, Hertz (Plate 4), British Airways and many others have established themselves as powerful marks around the world.

Differentiation

Most importantly, over the last few decades the way in which branded products or services have been distinguished from one another has increasingly concerned non-tangible factors rather than tangible factors or, at least, non-tangible factors have come to play an increasingly important rôle. One hundred years ago the emphasis was on getting the best, the freshest, the most innovative product to the consumer in order to capture his or her interest and, ultimately, allegiance. Nowadays most major international companies can match each other in terms of quality, freshness, innovation and so on. What, for example, makes most of the world drink Coca-Cola when in terms of taste and look and experience there may be little to choose from between it and a dozen other colas? The reason is the mix of tangible and intangible factors that combine to make Coca-Cola special in the eyes of consumers. Consumers today make brand choices upon an increasingly complex set of values, most of which are in many instances intangible.

Branding then has become a highly skilled and specialised discipline concerned with managing and maintaining a mix of factors, both tangible and intangible, that attract consumer loyalty. The art of successful branding lies in selecting and blending these elements so that the result is perceived by consumers to be uniquely attractive and influential on the purchasing decision.

Power Brands

Power brands are those brands which are particularly well adapted to the environment in which they operate and which thus survive and flourish. Power brands establish a strong 'pact' with consumers which competitor brands cannot match. Creating a power brand involves blending all of the elements of a brand in a unique way – the product or service must be of a high quality and be appropriate and relevant to the consumer's needs, the brand name must be appealing and in tune with the consumer's perception of the product, the packaging and visual identity must be attractive and distinctive and the pricing, support and advertising put behind the brand must meet similar tests of appeal, appropriateness and differentiation.

It is this last factor, differentiation, which is most frequently overlooked by brand owners. Any one of a dozen manufacturers could probably create a passable imitation of a Mars bar. These manufacturers would have to invest heavily in new equipment and, because they would not benefit from Mars' economies of scale, would have to sacrifice margin in order to meet Mars' price. None the less the Mars bar technology is not protected by any patent and it is quite possible that a competitor could produce a product which in taste, appearance and price could match that of a Mars bar.

Illustration I. 1

The Mars Bar has been a leading force in the world confectionery market since its launch in 1932. Its mix of brand values appeals to consumers across different national and cultural boundaries. Successful brand extension programmes into ice cream and milk have helped to build Mars into a genuine power brand.

Of course, Mars does have powerful legal rights which it can use to protect the brand from abuse or infringement – the Mars trade mark and all the supporting device mark registrations are protected at law and no competitor would be able to use them. But none of these rights could stop broad imitation of the Mars bar.

The reason why competitors seem unable to compete effectively with the Mars bar despite having the ability to match it in terms of taste, price and appearance is because the Mars bar has something extra which competitor brands do not. Consumers perceive that the mix of values represented by the Mars bar brand is uniquely attractive and different from anything else in the market. This differentiation is not achieved through the tangible aspects of the product – its taste, appearance or price – but through intangible factors such as its packaging, its name, its presentation and its brand personality. The Mars bar then has come to represent a whole mix of values and attributes which make it completely different from any other would-be imitator in the market. Mars stands for high quality, energy, activity, enthusiasm, fun, excitement and a whole host of other attractive and compelling values, all of which are sought after by consumers. Mars has genuine brand power.

Power brands have demonstrated that they can influence the market in which they operate. Mars completely revolutionised the ice-cream market when it introduced Mars bar ice-cream. Few other brands could have been used to such dramatic effect in creating an entirely new product category. Power brands generally occupy positions of market leadership – brands like Coca-Cola, Kodak, Marlboro, Sony and many others all lead their fields in terms of market share (see Illustration I.2). Power brands appeal to all kinds of consumer regardless of age, colour or background. The image of Pepsi or McDonald's is equally attractive to American kids as it is to European or Japanese teenagers. Power brands have also been established for a long time and have strong visually distinctive identities. The Coca-Cola script and dynamic curve, the Camel logo and the Marlboro chevron are internationally recognised symbols. Many of the world's biggest cigarette brands sponsor Formula One

SONY®

Illustration I. 2
Founded in 1946, Sony has become the world giant of the electronics industry. Innovative, focused and totally oriented towards the needs of the consumer, Sony has become one of the world's great power brands.

Grand Prix racing but find that they cannot use their brand names on Grand Prix cars because this would infringe local tobacco advertising regulations. The visual strength of brands like Marlboro and Camel means that consumers recognise the brand even if the name is not displayed.

Power brands are also generally supported consistently and powerfully by advertising and promotional initiatives. International campaigns for brands like Coca-Cola, American Express, Chanel, Ford and many others are very well known and have a relevance and an appeal to consumers all over the world. Power brands are equally at home in any country in the world and have proved their ability to cross cultural and geographic borders. Benetton, Campbell's, Nabisco and Nestlé have all established themselves as genuine power brands in this sense.

Brand Value

Power brands are also very valuable. The extraordinary resilience and security of demand evidenced by power brands represents a unique attraction to investors. An important issue surrounding brands today is not just how to create and market them, but to understand how others might perceive their success and, ultimately, their financial worth. Buying a power brand these days often makes much more economic sense than developing one through marketing, advertising, promotion and support over a number of non-profit-making years. It is well known that most new product development projects fail to capture the excitement of the market – for every successful new brand such as

Nintendo computer games there are a hundred or so also-rans which never achieve market success. It is far easier, therefore, to buy an established power brand with a strong consumer base than to try to create one from scratch.

Brands are increasingly regarded as tradeable assets of great worth, and during the 1980s this created an epidemic of takeover activity, with major household names changing hands for staggering sums of money. In just a few brief months in 1988, brands with an aggregate value of over $50 billion were bought and sold in just four deals:

(i)   RJR Nabisco, the tobacco, drink and foods group, was at the centre of a $25 billion fight between its management and the leveraged buy-out specialists, Kohlberg Kravis Roberts. The latter eventually won what was a very hostile takeover battle. Shortly after the deal was consummated Nabisco's European brands were sold to the French food giant BSN for $2.5 billion.

(ii)   American food and tobacco giant Philip Morris bought Kraft, the maker of the eponymous cheese products and a host of other brands including Miracle Whip toppings and Breyers ice-cream. The price was $12.9 billion, representing a sum over four times the worth of Kraft's tangible assets.

(iii)   Grand Metropolitan, the UK foods and spirits company, acquired Pillsbury for $5.5 billion, a sum which represented a 50 per cent premium to the American company's pre-bid market capitalisation and several times the value of its tangible assets.

(iv)   The Swiss multinational foods and beverages group Nestlé acquired Rowntree Mackintosh, the UK chocolate and confectionery maker with brands like Kit-Kat, Polo mints and After Eight, for $4.5 billion, a sum which at the time seemed to be excessive but which since then has been seen to have been one of the great deals of the decade.

Why have companies been prepared to spend such vast sums of money to acquire these portfolios of brands? The answer lies not only in the fact that it is much more difficult to develop a power brand from scratch than to buy it from someone else but also because power brands produce strong and highly reliable streams of cash flow. This, more than anything else, is what brand power is all about.

The Importance of Brands

Brands are important to brand owners at three quite different levels. First, they serve as a focus for consumer loyalties and therefore can be developed into assets which generate steady and reliable streams of cash flow. Brands therefore introduce stability into businesses and help to guard against competitive encroachment; they also allow planning and investment to take place with increased confidence.

Secondly, the brand serves to capture the promotional investment put into it. Enormously valuable brands like Kellogg's (Plate 5), Pepsi and Marlboro are still benefiting massively from the huge advertising spend they each received in the 1950s and 1960s when media costs were less than they were during the 1970s and 1980s. The benefits of past media spend accrue to brands for years afterwards. This ability to capture promotional investment is in direct contrast to what happens with generic goods or commodities, which have no brand name or image. A generic promotion for British cheese inevitably serves to stimulate interest in all cheese including German, French and Italian cheese and does not serve to create an enduring asset. On the other hand, a promotion for a branded cheese like Galbani's Bel Paese serves to promote the brand rather than the category (see Chapter 8 for more detail on how a commodity product like cheese can be successfully branded).

Finally, brands can be of critical strategic importance to their owners. In particular, brands enable manufacturers to communicate directly with consumers regardless of the actions of the middleman. This communication link is vital to the survival of many of the world's leading grocery companies. Without brands, such manufacturers would increasingly be at the mercy of retailers whose influence over the past ten years has grown dramatically.

The Threat of Own Label

Retailers in most developed countries have developed own label brands, sold only through their stores and without any manufacturer endorsement. These are not necessarily lower quality variants of branded products but in many cases are of equal quality but at a lower price. For decades manufacturers have turned a blind eye to this threat but many of the more complacent manufacturers are now facing serious difficulties. Many retailers will only stock one or two brands plus an own label variant for each product line in their stores. Frequently it is not economically viable to have more than two manufacturer brands per product line plus an own label version. This means, quite simply, that if you do not have a number one or number two brand your products will be delisted by leading retailers and, for many food manufacturers, this means disaster.

Manufacturers like Mars, Unilever, Procter & Gamble and BSN have managed to retain their share of shelf space by ensuring that each of their brands maintains a strong link with consumers. This has been achieved by strongly supporting the brands, ensuring that packaging, visual presentation, promotional offers and overall 'get-up' remain attractive and by continuing to manage all the various elements of the brand 'mix' so that the brands remain appealing to consumers.

The Importance of Brands to Consumers

Besides their importance to brand owners, brands are also important to consumers. A brand represents a pact between brand owner and consumer. Branding therefore is not a cynical activity imposed on the unsuspecting consumer against his or her will. Brands allow consumers to shop with confidence in what is an increasingly complex world. The brand offers the consumer a guarantee of quality, value and product satisfaction. As long as the brand keeps its part of the bargain the consumer will continue to support it.

Conversely, should the consumer not like the brand, or should it fail to deliver what the consumer requires, or should another brand appear which better suits the consumer's needs, then the brand's identity allows the consumer to avoid the brand and purchase an alternative.

The Features of a Power Brand

What then constitutes a power brand? The following features seem to be common to most power brands:

(i) At the core of the brand must lie strong intellectual property rights to which the brand's owner has clear legal title. Registered trade marks protecting the brand name itself are usually the key property rights in a brand but design rights, copyrights and patents may also contribute powerfully. (Kodak, for example, is a trademark of Eastman-Kodak which is registered on an international basis; the machines or the processes used to manufacture Kodak products may be protected by patent; the artwork on the packaging may be protected by copyright; and the shape of the container or general appearance of the product may be protected by design.) In the absence of intellectual property rights, brands cannot exist – they will merely be undifferentiated generics.

(ii) The brand must be meaningfully differentiated; it must stand apart from its competitors such that consumers recognise that the branded product has particular characteristics, both tangible and intangible. Unless brands are differentiated no brand personality can exist and the consumer has no reason to select any one brand in preference to another.

(iii) The brand must be appealing; the consumer must recognise the brand qualities and attributes which are desirable and which prompt recommendation and repurchase.

(iv) The brand must be consistent; it must continue to deliver satisfactions and must not let the consumer down.

(v) The brand must be supported through advertising or other forms of promotion and through distribution; the consumer must be aware of the brand and its qualities and it must, too, be available for the consumer to purchase.

(vi) The brand must address consumer needs which exist internationally; no brand can become international if the satisfactions it delivers are purely local in nature, and no purely national brand ever really achieves the status of a power brand.

(vii) Most importantly, the brand must be meticulously managed over an extended period of time: quality must be maintained, distribution ensured and competitive challenges met. And, as mentioned above, appropriate and appealing advertising and support is required, modified to suit changing needs and conditions; and consistent and appealing packaging must be used to help existing purchasers recognise the product as well as to attract new purchasers to it. Brand extension may also be required to exploit the 'equity' in the brand and keep the brand relevant and appealing but this, too, needs careful and skilful management.

What distinguishes the world's leading brands, both international and national, is the care and attention which are lavished on them by their owners. Good brand management requires single-mindedness, even a streak of fanaticism. All the great power brands display an attention to detail which sets them apart from the normal.

Benefits of Brand Power

Brand power provides security of demand and enables brand owners to generate strong and reliable streams of cash. Companies like Coca-Cola, Procter & Gamble, Unilever, Mars and Kodak have shown over many decades that they understand the meaning of brand power and have demonstrated their skill at using the power of brands to increase market share in existing markets, to expand into new markets and to increase returns to shareholders.

Recent Events

In April 1993 Philip Morris announced that it was to cut the price of Marlboro (Plate 6) in the USA to combat growing competition from discounters. Stock markets around the world were thrown into turmoil as a result of this news and billions of dollars were wiped off the value of some of the world's leading branded goods companies. The feeling was that if the great Marlboro brand was in trouble against cheap unbranded products then no brand could be safe.

The news of Marlboro's price cuts was followed in July 1993 with the announcement from Procter & Gamble that it was cutting the price of its detergents brands, Tide and Cheer, by 15 per cent. Then in Europe, the Chairman of BSN, the major French food manufacturer, stated that margins on its food brands were coming under increasing pressure. And in Britain reports continued to surface about the increasing share of own label brands at the expense of manufacturer's brands.

The above events have encouraged observers to suggest that the great days of the brands are over. My own view is that this concern over the future for brands is overdone. There are, of course, lessons to be learned from these recent events but they do not by any means represent the end of brand power.

The decision by Marlboro to reduce prices in the USA was brought about not because of any inherent defect in the brand but because the price of Marlboro was too high in relation to the rest of the market. For several years the price of Marlboro in the USA had been increased at a rate well in excess of inflation. This had led to a situation where discount brands were able to sell at half Marlboro's price and still make a decent return. This unusually large price discrepancy made it inevitable that consumers would start to drift towards cheaper substitutes. But Marlboro is not priced at such a large premium to the cheaper generic substitutes in all markets in the world. In the UK, for example, Marlboro is priced at a 26 per cent premium to the discount brands and in Germany at only an 8 per cent premium. In the UK and Germany it is far less likely that Marlboro will begin to lose share on price grounds alone. It seems that the price move initiated by Philip Morris was brought about by a unique set of circumstances affecting the US market.

The lesson to be learnt from the Marlboro experience (obvious though it may seem) is that pricing is a variable that must be watched very carefully – many brands are able to command a premium over generic substitutes but this must not be allowed to get out of control. In Marlboro's case it is a tribute to the strength of the brand that it was able to sustain such a large price premium for such a long time without losing too much share.

The decision by Procter & Gamble to reduce the pricing of Tide and Cheer can be rationalised in a similar manner. In 1992 Procter & Gamble launched its Every Day Low Pricing (EDLP) programme. Procter & Gamble felt that continuous price-based promotions were actually working against the long-term interest of its brands and that price promotion was becoming more important than brand loyalty. Promotions led to surges in demand which were difficult to plan and control. By lowering list prices Procter & Gamble was able to smooth out the wild fluctuations in demand caused by the constant stream of price promotions and refocus consumer interest on brand values as opposed to price.

BSN's comments about the threat of lower prices referred only to its tertiary brands – in fact its market leader brands are all robust and prices are holding up well. BSN's remarks, when taken in context, are no different from the comments being made by many other food manufacturers around the world. The fact is that the increased importance of own label brands and cheaper generics are forcing brand owners to focus their efforts on those brands that have the potential to become real power brands. Retaining a number three or four brand in one's portfolio, unless there are deliberate strategic reasons for this (such as constructing barriers to entry or utilising surplus capacity), is increasingly uneconomic. BSN intends to focus its efforts on its power brands such as

Danone, Evian, Lea & Perrins (Plate 7) and Kronenbourg rather than on continuing to support minor brands which are being forced to reduce prices to levels equal to or lower than own label brands in order to retain shelf space.

In Britain, in particular, the last dozen or so years has seen a substantial rise in retailer power with a huge proportion of the nation's grocery shopping being conducted through only six major retailers – Tesco, Marks & Spencer, Sainsbury's, Safeway, Gateway and ASDA. These retailers, and especially the first three, have shown themselves to be adept at spotting market opportunities in sectors where the branded manufacturers are weak, at developing new and improved products to meet these opportunities, sourcing these from suppliers who, in many cases, have no branded production and then at offering such products under their own brand names. In sectors such as frozen and chilled foods, ready prepared meals and baked products, own-label brands have frequently virtually driven out the manufacturer's brands, and own-labels are now the brands of choice of many consumers.

But this phenomenon does not signal the demise of the brand; rather it shows a new branding concept, own-label, taking over in areas where traditional branded suppliers have failed to keep their brands up to scratch. Indeed, such own-label brands are now true brands in every sense and are far from being merely cheap alternatives to the real thing. It is also noticeable that in sectors such as baby foods, instant coffee and breakfast cereals brand owners such as Heinz, Nestlé and Kellogg's have been not at all complacent and, as a result, own-label has made only very limited inroads.

Those forecasting the death of the brand have got it wrong. Brands provide owners with enormous benefits including more certain cash flows and, frequently, higher margins and even though price adjustments are bound to take place from time to time, this does not signal the end of brand power. It is also important to bear in mind that own-label branding is simply another form of branding, with the brand owner being the retailer rather than the manufacturer; it is not an alternative to branding. Right now, when many developed countries are still in recession, low-cost alternatives to established brands, whether own-label or otherwise, have their best opportunity in decades to claw back market share from the major manufacturer brands. We are not witnessing the death of the brand but evolutionary change. Clearly however in order to survive, the major brands must, as Procter & Gamble is doing, set the brand premium at an appropriate level and cut costs accordingly so as to maintain profitability.

Conclusion

Brand power is a phenomenon that requires very careful management. Owning a powerful brand cannot be taken to mean an absolute guarantee of future volumes and cash flow. On the contrary, brand power must be managed with meticulous attention to detail. Every element of the branding mix must be continually monitored and reviewed to ensure that it remains relevant and appealing to consumers. In the following chapters some of the world's great brand owners describe their own experience of brand power and how it has affected the way in which they manage their companies.

THE IMPORTANCE
OF BRAND POWER 1

Donald Keough
Former President and Chief Operating Officer
THE COCA-COLA COMPANY

I have never quite understood why people throughout the US marketing and advertising industry take so much delight in analysing the fate of those new products and brands that 'never get out of test market' or which 'die of consumer indifference'. Nor is this phenomenon restricted to the US – marketing people around the world spend a large amount of their time trumpeting the failure of new products, an activity which seems decidedly odd given that new product development is the responsibility of those same marketing people. Far too much time, money and effort is, in my view, invested in performing autopsies on products that fail and not nearly enough on examining, analysing, perhaps even celebrating, those brands that have succeeded year after year.

This book is dedicated to those brands that have stood the test of time. Among such power brands is one which continues to bring a smile to the faces of people around the world. That brand is Coca-Cola (see Plate 45).

Today, people in over 195 countries around the world can see the ubiquitous and powerful name of Coca-Cola, etched in white against a field of bright red. Travelling Americans are often surprised to see 'their Coke' in the hands of people who often have no idea that the brand's original birthplace is Atlanta, Georgia. Imagine the shock of American kids when a member of a junior baseball team visiting from Taiwan notices the bright red Coca-Cola scoreboard in centre field and says to his hosts, 'you have Coca-Cola in the US, too?' People regularly tell me stories of finding themselves in the most inaccessible parts of remote countries and yet being able to find a place that sells Coca-Cola. Coca-Cola has managed to transcend national boundaries to become one of the most powerful, and genuinely international, brands in the world.

Coca-Cola adds Life

In May 1886, Coca-Cola was offered to the public for the first time at Jacobs' Pharmacy in Atlanta, Georgia. The price was five cents a glass. At virtually the same time the Government of France made a gift to the USA of the Statue of Liberty, a symbol which was to become one of the most powerful icons of American culture. Indeed, many of the qualities associated with the Statue of Liberty such as freedom, democracy, equality and a new beginning, are all qualities that have come too to be linked with Coca-Cola. How appropriate that Coca-Cola celebrated its 100th birthday at the same time as the Statue of Liberty.

Coca-Cola is now well into its second century of life. Business students and many marketing consultants would have us believe that all products have finite life cycles. It is said that all products go through the following phases: *Introduction*; *Acceptance*; *Growth*; *Maturity*; and *Decline*. But which stage is Coca-Cola at according to this life cycle? The brand is already 107 years old and is still being introduced into many countries, still winning acceptance in new markets, and still growing in existing markets around the world. It is by no means 'mature', and certainly not declining. According to Audits & Surveys, Inc, Americans consume more than 100 million cans, bottles or glasses of Coca-Cola a day. If we include the 33 countries outside the USA also measured by Audits and Surveys' international consumer study, the total is more than 250 million drinks a day. If we also add consumption in the other 161 countries where Coca-Cola is enjoyed, total daily consumption probably exceeds half a billion.

What is Brand Power?

Brand power is a quality possessed by only the strongest international brands. A power brand is characterised by the distinctive nature of its brand personality, by the appeal and relevance of its image, by the consistency of its communication, by the integrity of its identity and by the fact that it has stood the test of time. But, of course, power brands have to evolve so as to remain contemporary for each new generation of consumers. What appeals to the young of today may be very different from that which appealed to the young of the 1920s, 1940s or 1960s. Power brands also have to convey subtly different messages to different consumer groups within the same market. Coca-Cola may mean fun, adventure and liveliness to young people, but it has slightly softer overtones to the 'thirty-somethings'.

The brand also has to work in different ways from market to market. In the USA, Coca-Cola is the quintessential American soft drink, with powerful associations of freedom, liberty and the American dream. This positioning would not have precisely the same appeal to consumers in the UK, so the brand's personality has been shifted for the UK consumer to focus more on the fun-loving, good-time connotations of the brand, with much less emphasis on its 'US' origins. And in any case, Europeans do not generally see Coca-Cola as a US product – they see it as relevant to and part of their own culture and environment.

Although I am convinced that Coca-Cola has all the attributes of a power brand and that it may well be the world's most powerful brand, I am not so sure that anyone at the Coca-Cola Corporation should be entirely comfortable with the term itself. Believing a brand to be all-powerful inevitably leads to complacency, which can have damaging consequences for the brand. We need constantly to keep a close eye on our brand management techniques and we need continuously to promote the Coca-Cola brand in a consistent and robust manner, in order to ensure that the brand has a long and happy future. Our brand power comes from the people we have involved in the production, distribution,

Illustration 1.1

Making Coca-Cola available to people everywhere requires enormous investment in distribution and logistics. Coca-Cola's international distribution system is one of the most sophisticated in the world and often has to use unusual means of transportation such as this barge that regularly crosses Brazil's Amazon river with a full cargo of Coca-Cola.

marketing and management of the brand. It also comes, of course, from the consumers of Coca-Cola.

One of the most important factors behind Coca-Cola's success is a production and distribution system that ensures the product reaches consumers in perfect condition wherever they may be in the world. Some 20 000 associates and almost one million men and women help to make the Coca-Cola production and distribution system work. The system also provides technical and logistical support for product formulation, product manufacturing techniques, quality control procedures, distribution, design, packaging technology and marketing strategy. The amount of time, expertise and investment behind the Coca-Cola product is unmatched anywhere in the world. There is no substitute for the Coca-Cola product offer – it *is* 'the real thing'.

This concept of ultimate superiority defines the essence of Coca-Cola's brand power. Consumers accept and recognise

Illustration 1.2
  Valentine La Chica, a 73-year-old Filipino, sells cold Coca-Cola for at least twelve
  hours every day, refusing to leave the market place until he has sold fifty cases. It is
  this sort of dedication from everyone involved in the supply chain that enables the
  Coca-Cola distribution system to work effectively.

Coca-Cola as the ultimate in terms of quality. The advertising strap line 'the real thing' is seen by consumers as a totally credible statement about the brand's virtues. What reinforces this conviction amongst consumers, apart from the reassurance provided by the consistent quality of the Coca-Cola product, is that competitive brands all seek to emulate Coca-Cola. There is very little attempt on their part to create a distinctive positioning and personality for their brands. Because Coca-Cola already occupies the Number One position, the competition must find a way to get round the fact that, for consumers, Coke is the real thing. Their approach, in the main, has been to attempt to convince consumers that their product tastes exactly the same as Coca-Cola. For decade after decade Coca-Cola has maintained its market leadership, never losing the high ground to a competitor, and competitive activity has consistently reinforced the truth of Coca-Cola's leadership claims.

That no other soft drink has ever approached the market leadership of Coca-Cola is a tribute to the strength and power of the brand. The power of any brand derives from a complex combination of factors, including the strength of its positioning and personality, the relevance and appeal of its image, the quality of the product it endorses, the service support behind it and the effectiveness of its marketing strategy.

No one has ever been able to duplicate the Coca-Cola brand. A vast, complex network of production, distribution and marketing has kept the brand in front. Of course, there are many markets in the world where the battle for leadership is fierce and Coca-Cola's ownership of it stubbornly contested. Nevertheless, in all but a handful of countries, the lead enjoyed by Coca-Cola is significant.

Maintaining Leadership through Brand Management

Maintaining Coca-Cola's dominance around the world is achieved by paying constant and meticulous attention to brand management. The international network that provides Coca-Cola with so much of the support it needs to remain ahead of the competition is, as we have seen, the brand's true powerhouse. Coca-Cola bottlers around the world get the Coca-Cola product to consumers in 195 countries. Wherever people happen to be, whether it is on the beach, in the office, eating out at a restaurant or at home in front of the television, Coca-Cola is there. Coca-Cola's presence, visibility and availability in the market is unequalled by any other soft drink brand anywhere. It can lay claim to being the most visible brand in the world.

The Coca-Cola system ensures that Coca-Cola is everywhere. Presence, availability, visibility, are the goals of that system. The machinery, the vehicles and the people that make up this system are a key element of Coca-Cola's brand power.

The Power of Presence

Coca-Cola is labelled the best-known brand name in the world. It is variously called the most respected brand name in the world, the most recognised, the most familiar, the most popular, the most international, the most esteemed, the most friendly, the most asked for, the most reproduced, the most enviable and the most loved. But there are, of course, often less flattering tributes to the brand's ubiquity. Predictably, makers of other beverages, for example, do not welcome the availability and visibility of Coca-Cola in their markets. And who would expect them to? Yet, all the red and white advertising signs, the red trucks and vending machines, the fountain dispensers and retail identity signs, the menu boards and box coolers, the red sun visors and the T-shirts, and all

Illustration 1.3
In 1971, young people from around the world gathered on a hilltop in Italy to sing 'I'd like to buy the world a Coke'. A symbol of the early 1970s, this commercial became one of the most famous in The Coca-Cola Company's history.

the red cans and red-labelled bottles stacked within reach of anyone choosing to enjoy a Coca-Cola – all of these things ensure that Coca-Cola is never far from the consumer's consciousness.

Great brands need frequent and consistent advertising to make and keep them great. The highly popular advertising campaigns that have helped to make Coca-Cola great are among the most exciting, innovative and powerful advertisements ever made. I am an ardent believer in the power of advertising and The Coca-Cola Company is probably one of the world's biggest buyers of it. But competitors also advertise. Their efforts normally attempt to evoke the same qualities and personality that Coca-Cola already conveys. But what competitors cannot match and where Coca-Cola continues to win is in its overwhelming presence. Advertising certainly awakens or re-awakens consumer interest in particular brands and informs consumers about brand quality, desirability and image, but I believe that brand presence closes the sale.

Illustration 1.4
Japan has one of the largest markets in the world for vending machines. The Coca-Cola Company has placed nearly 800 000 vending machines throughout Japan, including this one in a Tokyo train station.

Throughout America, and indeed throughout the world, there are tens of thousands of soft drink outlets contracted to sell Coca-Cola's products. A list of all the restaurant chains, hotels, airlines, sports stadiums, theme parks, universities, country clubs and cinemas which serve Coca-Cola would fill the remainder of this book. It is enough to say that consumers have come to expect Coca-Cola wherever they may be in the world, and we do not let them down.

When consumers watch a film, they expect to see the actors quenching their thirst with a Coke. Conversely, when consumers see competitors' vending machines and signage in such films, or hear actors ask for something other than Coke, I suspect they are just as surprised as they would be to discover that a restaurant or hotel in the real world did not serve Coca-Cola.

In 195 countries around the world, the presence of Coca-Cola is an increasing part of life. The power of presence is evident in increased volume and steadily increasing per

Illustration 1.5
The range of products sold by the Coca-Cola company are sold in virtually every country in the world. Here, a street vendor outside Beijing in China is seen selling a range of Coca-Cola products.

capita consumption. It is extraordinary how this brand can take root and thrive in countries that once seemed to care little about soft drinks, much less boast a 'cola culture'. Mature brand? Hardly. Coca-Cola's future is in front of it.

Brand Expansion

The opportunity for Coke to expand is still enormous. Consumers in Eastern Europe are embracing Coca-Cola as a brand in sympathy with their new-found freedom. Coca-Cola celebrates freedom and is literally bubbling with optimism. It is the perfect brand for consumers wishing to find their way in the free world. The Coca-Cola Company is investing hundreds of millions of dollars to ensure that Coca-Cola's presence is as strong in these new democracies as it is elsewhere in the world. Such investment in new machinery, distribution, advertising and in people has not only enabled Coca-Cola to enter new markets but has also provided developing market economies with much-needed jobs. In many parts of the world, this economic lift offered by Coca-Cola is every bit as welcome as the sheer physical enjoyment of the product.

The excellence of our products, the quality of our people, the strength and growth of our presence around the world will always be essential to Coca-Cola's continuing success. But the most important source of Coca-Cola's brand power does not derive from the bottlers, the Coca-Cola system, the corporation itself, its executive committees, employees, boards of directors, company presidents or chief executives. It derives from the consumer.

Brand Power Resides in the Hands of Consumers

In May 1985, a year before Coca-Cola celebrated its 100th birthday, the company announced that it was removing the original formula product from the market and replacing it with a new, improved product. This new, improved product

Illustration 1.6
On May 15, 1950 Coca-Cola appeared on the front cover of *Time* magazine. This edition of the magazine featured a story about the worldwide success and ubiquity of Coca-Cola.

would be marketed under the Coca-Cola and Coke brand names.

The company's rationale for this action was that prolonged product development work, involving significant amounts of consumer research, had produced a new product that was not only superior to competitor products but was also superior to the original Coke. The new product had done so well in testing and in research that the company felt an obligation to offer it to consumers.

Consumer response to the announcement and to the new product was immediate and overwhelming. Consumers made more than 400 000 blistering phone calls to the company and its network of bottlers and wrote some 200 000 letters and post cards, all decrying the proposal to remove the old formula Coke. Societies and action groups were formed and all of them used the figure of a sad, unsmiling face to characterise their literature.

In response to such overwhelming consumer demand, The Coca-Cola Company brought the old formula Coca-Cola back just as fast as it had taken it away: it was launched under the name Coca-Cola Classic. Every television news broadcast, every front page of America's – and many of the world's – daily newspapers and every radio station carried the refreshing news. The only cola war anyone cared about was over. The consumer had won. Coca-Cola Classic was coming home.

The jubilation of consumers at this news was immense. Consumer power had spoken out to reclaim the integrity and heritage of the brand. The launch of Coca-Cola Classic marked the beginning of another period of sustained growth for the Coca-Cola family of brands. The new formula Coke increased its share dramatically, and Coca-Cola Classic saw its share grow exponentially as loyal consumers flocked to the original formula product. It became one of the most successful line extensions ever. New Coke, now marketed as Coke II, still refreshes millions of consumers in the USA.

Line Extensions

Another line extension that has exceeded our wildest dreams has been the launch and subsequent success of Diet Coke. Now in its eleventh year, this new line extension has been spectacularly successful in matching the desire of millions of consumers for the same sense of fun and enjoyment delivered by the regular Coca-Cola brand, but with fewer calories. Diet Coke is now the third best-selling soft drink in the world.

The 'Pact' between Consumer and Manufacturer

It is difficult to imagine a more difficult and fragile relationship than that which exists between consumer and manufacturer. The continuing need to reassure consumers about the consistency and quality of the product creates intense demands. The relationship has to be carefully monitored. Advertising, promotion and sponsorship activ-

Illustration 1.7
For several decades, Haddon Sundblom's energetic and refreshing Sprite illustration was a signature for Coca-Cola around the world. Coca-Cola has always invested heavily in advertising and promotion in support of the brand.

ities all have to be managed sensitively and appropriately to ensure that the messages communicated to consumers are, and remain, relevant and appealing. The manufacturer cannot afford to make a mistake with his communication strategy, since consumers are quick to let you know their feelings – usually by switching to a competitive brand.

The relationship between The Coca-Cola Corporation and its consumers around the world is fundamental to the power of the Coca-Cola brand. The experience of Coca-Cola Classic has reinforced our commitment to satisfying consumer needs, however these may vary globally. The great advantage for Coca-Cola in this regard is that the values and qualities that consumers associate with Coca-Cola are very similar, whether they live in Northern Finland or on the South Island of New Zealand. Yet it is an immense task to maintain a strong relationship with consumers when they are literally all round the world – it requires the concerted efforts of tens of thousands of Coca-Cola personnel and hundreds of

Illustration 1.8
In July 1985 Coca-Cola became the first soft drink to be enjoyed in outer space, as Commander Gordon Fullerton and his fellow astronauts aboard the shuttle Challenger tested a space can developed by The Coca-Cola Company.

millions of advertising dollars. The relationship with our consumers is as strong today as it has ever been, and we are finding new consumers with whom to communicate in Eastern Europe and the new independent states of the former USSR.

The relationship between Coca-Cola and its consumers is one of the reasons for the brand's success. Coca-Cola's local presence gives it a close personal relationship with the communities it serves. When Coca-Cola sponsors a local event, an athletic team, or a civic project, it is Coca-Cola people who actually pitch in and help. I believe that one key reason why consumers remain so loyal to Coca-Cola is the fact that the brand and the support behind it in terms of Coca-Cola people, sponsorship programmes and community initiatives are always right around the corner. Consumers believe that Coca-Cola cares about the communities it serves and is always on hand to help. But in spite of all such analysis and hypothesising neither I nor any cultural historian, marketing analyst or monitor of consumer trends has ever explained – to my satisfaction – the mysterious emotional bond that so many people have with Coke.

Andy Warhol may have said it best in his book *The Philosophy of Andy Warhol (from A to B and Back Again)*:

> What's great about this country is that America started the tradition where the richest consumers buy essentially the same things as the poorest. You can be watching TV and see Coca-Cola, and you can know that the President drinks Coke, Liz Taylor drinks Coke, and just think, you can drink Coke too. A Coke is a Coke and no amount of money can get you a better Coke than the one the bum on the corner is drinking. All Cokes are the same and all Cokes are good. Liz Taylor knows it, the President knows it, the bum knows it and you know it.

People around the world actually have shared their happiest times – love, laughter and celebration – in the companionship of Coke. Coca-Cola is simply a part of life. Perhaps, in the end, that is the real secret of brand power.

Illustration 1.9
Like millions of other Americans, former President John F. Kennedy also enjoyed Coca-Cola.

CREATING BRAND POWER 2

Sir Anthony Tennant
Former Chairman
GUINNESS PLC

At first glance, **creating** brand power may seem an unusual subject for the former Chairman of Guinness plc. After all, the vast majority of the brands in our comprehensive portfolio date back to the last century or even beyond. Guinness Stout (Plate 8), the famous dark brew, traces its origins to 1759, the year the company was founded in Dublin. Guinness is thus in the enviable position of owning brand names which have already established a powerful reputation. The real challenge for Guinness is to maintain and extend that brand power. We have, accordingly, maintained a very tight focus on our core spirits and beer brands. It is a fundamental objective of our corporate strategy to concentrate on our core brands and to develop and maintain their strength in all our markets around the world.

What is a Brand?

At its most basic level, a brand is a sign of identification, the label which differentiates your product from those of your competitors. A brand can also act as a type of shorthand encapsulating the key features of the product, such as its image, use and price, in an easily recognised and remembered form. A brand name is particularly important for **functional products** which operate in such market sectors as household goods, motor oil and stationery, where rival

Illustration 2.1
Guinness was first brewed by Arthur Guinness at his Dublin brewery in the 1750s and is now a major world brand brewed in Ireland, England, West Africa, Asia and even the Bahamas. Through skilful marketing the brand has remained relevant and appealing to many generations of consumers.

brands all perform the same practical purpose and there is little, other than the name, to distinguish between them.

But the brand or label given to a **representational** product is also important. Consumers purchase perfumes, Scotch whisky and luxury cars not so much for their practical purpose, but more for the inherent qualities and image they project. Clearly, these intangible messages can say as much about the purchaser as about the product.

Of course, most brands are neither purely representational nor purely functional. Many are a mixture of the two, with one or the other dominating. Within Guinness our business is in the main to market premium, aspirational brands successfully and profitably. For this reason I shall concentrate on representational brands, for, whilst our brands do have an important functional rôle, it is ultimately their representational qualities which attract the consumer.

Brands are a marketing company's most important assets. Witness the current trend to recognise the capital value of brands in company balance sheets. In the drinks industry, it is our experience that consumers in many countries are drinking less in volume terms but are shifting towards the purchase of more premium brands. In effect, they are drinking less but drinking better. This shift has been brought about not only because of an attraction to products of high quality, but also because of the more desirable brand images of these premium products.

Why Brand at all?

Some people ask 'why brand at all?' After all, merely applying a label to a product, as with many supermarket 'own labels', rather than investing in building a brand, would frequently result in much reduced costs. But, this would leave the consumer in many instances with no means of choice between alternative products other than on the basis of price. Such a strategy would certainly allow no room for premium brands and would result in most products assuming commodity status. It would also greatly reduce the richness, interest and diversity in our lives.

Fortunately, the powerful recent growth in own label branding has been matched in many instances by an ever-increasing demand for luxury, premium products. Furthermore, it is our view that the rise in popularity of top quality products is a trend likely to continue. Today's consumer is much more sophisticated than his counterpart of thirty or even twenty years ago. Such consumers are more likely to demand high quality and image and are finding increasingly that they have the means to purchase premium brands. Moreover, attainable luxury is very important to the discerning consumer – whilst one may not be able to afford a Porsche, by purchasing premium Scotch or by wearing Dior or Armani clothes one is able to enjoy and project a certain desirable image and to make a definitive statement about the quality of one's lifestyle and aspirations.

What Makes a Powerful Brand?

The most important attribute of a successful brand is, of course, the *product* itself. Creating a brand image for a product which does not match the consumer's expectations is a formula for certain failure. On the other hand, a product which lives up to its image or even surpasses it, has a definite headstart regardless of market conditions.

The second most important component of a brand is its *personality*. A consumer must feel comfortable with a brand, must feel an affinity with it and must feel that the brand has certain relevant qualities to offer. A brand's personality thus embodies all of the qualities it has to offer over and above its primary characteristics and its functional purpose. It is also crucial that a brand's personality should never be seen perceptibly to change but, rather, that it should only ever be seen to evolve over time.

The third factor of critical significance to a successful brand is that of providing a consistent *guarantee* of quality and consistency. With a good product, a distinctive brand personality and a consistently high quality offer, the brand owner is well placed to develop a successful and valuable brand asset.

Creating New Brands

New products are developed and launched, often at huge cost, in order to generate extra profits. Such new products, properly conceived and managed, can be startlingly successful, especially when a new category is created, as was the case, for instance, with Baileys Irish Cream. Indeed, in today's competitive marketplace there are many advantages to be gained from developing new brands. Conversely, the task of revitalising an existing brand which has been performing badly is often dauntingly difficult, given the need to reverse those negative perceptions which have built up. But with a new brand a marketeer can, in effect, start with a clean slate.

Nowadays virtually every large branded goods company spends huge sums of money on new product development. Unfortunately, however, original ideas are very few and far between, a situation which is often made worse by the fact that companies competing in the same marketplace usually use the same research techniques and are likely to read the same journals, and so identify and introduce similar products. True differentiation of product type and formulation, positioning and personality is notoriously difficult to achieve.

Developing a new brand is also extremely costly, a not unimportant factor in today's harsher economic climate. New products often divert effort and cash from existing mainstream brands and, in any case, over 80 per cent of new products fail after launch. With such poor odds, it is vital that every new product is thoroughly researched to establish that a market opportunity really does exist and is then carefully test marketed so that consumer responses to the new product can be fully assessed.

Line extensions are becoming an increasingly popular method of extending or 'leveraging' brand power. A brand with a successful personality lends itself to the development of line extensions as, in many instances, it is much easier to capitalise on a winning formula than to create a new brand from scratch. The chances of success are often greatly increased by building on an established brand.

Illustration 2.2

Tanqueray Gin, the number one imported gin in the US market, was used to support the introduction of Tanqueray Sterling Vodka – the Tanqueray name had strong associations of quality for American consumers and this no doubt helped to make the launch of Tanqueray Sterling Vodka such a success.

A good example of a successful brand extension is the development of Mars ice cream bars. Mars noticed a gap in the ice cream market and filled it by capitalising on the name, formulation and personality of its flagship brand. In doing so Mars has created a new super-premium ice cream category. The combination of an excellent product and the imagery attached to the Mars name meant that advertising of the new product was hardly necessary. Without doubt, the success of this brand owes a very great deal to the appeal and popularity of the original brand.

A new line extension can therefore enjoy an edge over competing brands if it is appropriately matched to the original's successful name and personality. However, the image and personality of the brand extension must be carefully controlled so as not to cause damage to the parent. Properly handled, sales of the parent brand may actually improve as a result of the extra shelf space set aside for the new brand extension as well as from the publicity attached to the launch of the brand extension.

Line extensions, particularly premium line extensions, play an important rôle in Guinness' brand-building strategy – they allow the consumer to trade up, to aspire to higher premium brands within their favourite range. They also provide us with the means of capturing consumer loyalty. For example, in 1990, United Distillers in the USA capitalised on the name of Tanqueray Gin, the number one imported gin, to support the launch of a new premium brand – Tanqueray Sterling Vodka. The Tanqueray name was already well known to American consumers, who recognised it as a guarantee of quality, and there is little doubt that the success of Tanqueray Sterling Vodka is in large part due to its association with the original Tanqueray Gin brand.

But perhaps the most notable 'super premium' line extensions we have introduced over the last few years have been to the Johnnie Walker and Old Parr brands. Old Parr Elizabethan, for example, is the most expensive Scotch whisky in the world and retails at $850 a bottle.

Illustration 2.3
Old Parr Elizabethan is the most expensive Scotch in the world, retailing at $850 a bottle.

Increasing Brand Power

Advertising, promotion and sponsorship are all vital to the building of brand power. However, it is crucial that all these activities are carried out in a *focused* way. It is important not to underestimate the effect that unfocused or inappropriate advertising can have in diluting brand power. Such advertising can severely damage a brand's image or personality to the extent that it may never recover.

Another important reason for 'getting it right' is the ever increasing cost of advertising and sponsorship. Work done in building a brand should not be carried out in a haphazard fashion, thereby wasting resources. Proper research and careful test marketing are vital to ensure that the risks of brand dilution are reduced to the minimum.

In the area of sponsorship, for example, it is important to target such sponsorship precisely. United Distillers, the spirits company of Guinness plc, is closely involved in golf sponsorship through events such as the Johnnie Walker

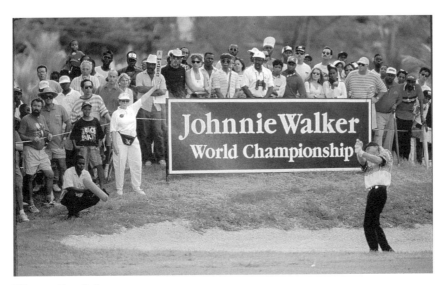

Illustration 2.4
Johnnie Walker plays a major role in the sponsorship of golf. Here Greg Norman, one of the world's leading golfers, is shown playing at the 1992 Johnnie Walker World Championship trophy.

Ryder Cup, the Johnnie Walker World Championship and the Bell's Scottish Open. Clearly, the image of golf makes the right lifestyle statement about Scotch whisky consumers, but such sponsorship would not be appropriate for Draught Guinness, which has a completely different image and target audience and which chooses instead to sponsor events such as rugby, horse racing and soccer.

Illustration 2.5
  The craftsmanship and skill taken in the production and preparation of Dewars ensures that the brand's reputation for quality is maintained.

The Guinness Experience

Background

The recent experience of Guinness plc provides a useful case study of the creation, extension and capitalisation of brand power.

With the acquisition of the Distillers Company in 1986, Guinness plc, producers of the famous creamy stout, inherited a large number of quality spirits brands including Johnnie Walker (the world's number one Scotch), Bells (the number one Scotch in the UK), Dewar's (number one Scotch in the USA), White Horse (number one Scotch in Japan), Gordon's Gin (number one gin worldwide) and of course, Pimm's, a brand which is in a class of its own.

The Distillers Company had been run as a large number of separate and largely autonomous brand companies and the marketing of the various spirits brands around the world had been left to local distributors who handled more than 75 per cent of each company's volume. Unfortunately, some major brands were losing market share as a result of a lack of a consistent and coherent image across their various markets.

In the post-acquisition period Guinness recognised that, if the potential brand power of the Distillers' portfolio was to be realised, the acquired businesses would need substantial reorganisation and restructuring. The first important step in the reorganisation of United Distillers (as it became known) was to gain direct involvement in the distribution and marketing of Guinness brands. This was achieved in three ways, as described below.

Joint ventures

Through a series of joint venture agreements and acquisitions, effective management of marketing and distribution was achieved.

The most important of these joint ventures was that agreed between United Distillers and the French company LVMH

Moët Hennessy Louis Vuitton. LVMH is one of France's leading companies and is, like United Distillers, a marketeer of premium, luxury goods. LVMH's brands include Hine and Hennessy Cognacs and Moët & Chandon, Mercier, Pomméry and Dom Perignon Champagnes. The relationship between the two companies began in 1987 when arrangements were made to distribute both companies' spirits portfolios in key markets such as Japan and the USA through one distribution company; today, United Distillers and LVMH have fourteen joint venture agreements.

The benefits to be derived from uniting, in distribution terms at least, the impressive portfolios of United Distillers and LVMH are clear. Separately, each enjoys leadership in its respective spirits categories – LVMH in Champagne and Cognac, and United Distillers in Scotch whisky and gin. Individually, each company enjoys considerable depth but insufficient breadth fully to exploit its potential. By uniting the two portfolios in certain markets, we have managed to increase greatly our marketing and distribution strength.

Together the two companies have an unrivalled portfolio of quality brands. The respective portfolios of premium gin, Scotch, Cognac and Champagne complement each other well. To date, this relationship has brought considerable benefits to both partners in terms of economies of scale and improved reach. To reinforce this relationship, Guinness and LVMH have taken shareholdings in each other's share capital.

In addition United Distillers has established a number of other joint venture partnerships with companies like Bacardi and Codorniu in Spain, Bacardi and Underberg in Germany, Real Companhia Velha in Portugal and Boutari in Greece.

But as well as establishing such joint venture agreements, Guinness has also acquired several businesses during the last few years and this has enabled the marketing and distribution of our brands to be brought back under our direct supervision. In 1986, over 75 per cent of United Distillers' sales were made through third-party distributors and agents; today that figure has fallen to less than 20 per cent.

There are those who argue that joint venture arrangements are inherently unstable, that it is difficult to fulfil the needs of both partners without sacrificing individual requirements.

Obviously, joint ventures do not come without risk, but if partners are chosen carefully, have complementary portfolios and secure equal benefits from the arrangements, they are likely to succeed. Problems arise if partners' portfolios overlap or compete with each other, or if the groundwork which precedes such an arrangement has not been thoroughly carried out.

But it is not only United Distillers which has been able to derive significant benefits from joint venture arrangements. Guinness Brewing Worldwide, the company charged with the management of the Guinness brand, the only leading international beer which is not a lager, has also benefited from joint ventures, a process aided by the fact that it is not perceived as a competitor to blond beers but rather as a natural partner. This, coupled with GBW's long-established marketing experience and presence in over 120 markets, makes Guinness the logical choice of partner for other premium brewers. One such of these joint ventures is with Heineken in Malaysia; other Guinness Brewing partners include Anheuser-Busch, Carlsberg and Labatt.

Revitalisation of brand image

United Distillers has also improved the power of its brands by revitalising the images of many of its top brands which, under the old Distillers stewardship, had suffered from inconsistent marketing across different parts of the world. We embarked upon a thorough programme of consumer research to get the marketing of these brands back on track and then invested heavily in targeted marketing spend to re-establish the brand power of the portfolio.

The 'whisky loch'

We also had to address early on the serious problems created by the 'whisky loch', a massive build-up of surplus whisky stock, a situation which plagued the Scotch industry during the early to mid 1980s. The dumping of surplus whisky by companies over this period led to the creation of a large number of cheap secondary whisky products and 'sub-norms' which took sales from the established brands and which seriously degraded the image of Scotch whisky. Moreover, the Scotch whisky industry made a further grave error when it reduced the price of regular branded products in the mistaken belief that this would stimulate consumption. During the 1980s, the price of Scotch halved in real terms in the USA, resulting in a considerable reduction in the status of Scotch. Over the same period Cognac's image continued to improve while Scotch was fast becoming a commodity product, its value being determined by price alone.

Such a fate clearly did not fit a quality product such as Scotch whisky, the heritage and craftsmanship of which merits equal status with Cognac or Champagne and the eventual drying up of the 'whisky loch' left an enormous amount of rehabilitation work to be done. United Distillers' task was to help raise the profile and image of Scotch whisky and thus repair the damage.

Obviously, this was not something we could achieve overnight. Comprehensive consumer research, significant investment in product quality, consistent advertising and the recruitment of the ablest people in the business were just a few of the measures which were necessary. But over the last few years, through a sustained effort, we have been able to draw attention to the inherent quality, image and status of Scotch whisky and restore the drink's status in the eyes of consumers.

Recreating Brand Power – Johnnie Walker

Johnnie Walker is the world's best selling Scotch whisky. However, in the middle of the 1980s its share of the global Scotch whisky market began to decline.

The revitalisation of the Johnnie Walker brand was crucial to the strengthening of the United Distillers portfolio. Our first action in 1987 was to create a Johnnie Walker global steering committee charged with the task of revitalising the brand, and comprising the brand director, research and

Illustration 2.6

> Johnnie Walker is the world's best-selling Scotch whisky. The brand is used to endorse a number of products, the most famous of which are the Red and Black Label sub-brands.

planning director, United Distillers' regional directors, the advertising agency, packaging design agency and research agencies. We felt that this vital task had to be centrally controlled, at least until a global strategy had emerged.

The steering committee's first action was to commission a full review and analysis of all existing knowledge on Johnnie Walker in both its Red and Black Label manifestations. This analysis demonstrated that the brands' decline could not be explained away by the previous management's decisions to change distribution and pricing. All the signs were that there was something seriously wrong with the brand's image. Consumer perceptions of the brand had changed and Scotch drinkers were beginning to move away from Red and Black Label.

This led us to set up a major examination of both brands at the consumer level. Given the complex nature of brand imagery and personality, we employed trained psychologists to talk to Johnnie Walker consumers, as well as to consumers of competitive brands, in Johnnie Walker's fourteen key markets. The results of this comprehensive study revealed the problem quite clearly: a serious and growing mismatch had developed between consumer needs and desires on the one hand and what the Johnnie Walker brand offered on the other. Much of the brand's image problem had come about through inappropriate and ill-judged advertising and promotional activity. The most encouraging aspect of the analysis and the research was, however, that despite the lacklustre management of the brand, it still retained a set of core values which were recognised across the world.

From this 'Essence of Johnnie Walker' study, as it became known, we were able to prepare a clear and unambiguous statement of how both the Red and Black Label brands should be positioned. We took decisions on advertising strategy, pack design and price positioning. All overt manifestations of both brands were re-examined and re-specified so that they were consistent in supporting and reinforcing the core values of the brands.

Obviously, the process of repositioning and revitalising the Johnnie Walker brands around the world took time – two years just for the first development phase. It also required enormous amounts of research and test marketing. Each new brand element, including the label design, price, personality, advertising and sponsorship, was thoroughly tested to ensure that what we had created totally fulfilled the wants and needs of our consumers.

We found that though we were able to use the same improved pack design around the world, and the same (old but loved) product, we had to tailor our advertising to meet the needs of local markets and cultures. Thus today we have separate campaigns in the USA, Latin America, UK, Europe, Africa, Japan, Thailand and Australia, but they are all based on the same set of core values. In their own culturally-specific way each of these advertising campaigns relays the same message to the consumer in his or her own advertising language.

Johnnie Walker is today once again on the ascent and has consolidated its number-one status on a global basis.

Canned Draught Guinness

The development of the Draught Guinness in cans product is neither a true new product development nor a brand extension; rather it is more of a product innovation.

At the beginning of the 1980s, the take-home beer market in the UK was growing rapidly. Increased ownership of video recorders and CD players reflected the increase in popularity of home entertainment and of socialising at home rather than in pubs and restaurants. However, consumers knew that the beers they drank at home were not the same as those sold in pubs and restaurants and, in particular, there were no true take-home draught beers.

Guinness Brewing saw a real gap in the market, a gap it could fill if the unique taste of Draught Guinness could be genuinely 'captured' in a can. To be successful, the canned version would have to pass a critical consumer test – if the consumer could not differentiate between Draught Guinness and the canned version, then the product would be a success.

On the face of it, it was an impossible task because by their very nature, draught beers must be served from a keg or a barrel. What Guinness Brewing had to do therefore was create a miniature keg that was capable of delivering the

Illustration 2.7

With the growth of the take home market in the UK, Guinness Brewing set out to develop a canned Guinness product that tasted the same as Draught Guinness. A unique in-can system was developed which produced the same surge, head and taste of the draught product but out of a can. The new product proved an outstanding success

characteristic unique creamy head and smooth taste of Draught Guinness. Furthermore, research indicated that whilst there were seven million Guinness drinkers in the

UK, the majority of Draught Guinness drinkers did not drink Guinness Original (that is, the bottled product), so there was little danger of cannibalising an already substantial take-home brand.

Over 100 packaging devices were tested before the unique in-can system was developed. This patented device, located at the bottom of the can, works ingeniously to reproduce the unique surge, head and taste of real Draught Guinness. The pressure change caused by opening the can forces dissolved gases out into the chamber at the bottom, pushing nitrogen and carbon dioxide bubbles through the beer in the can, thus recreating the famous creamy head when the Guinness is poured into a glass. The ingenuity of this technology was acknowledged by the accolade of the Queens Award for Technology.

Once a means had been found to reproduce Draught Guinness, the next job was to research the market potential for it. Consumers were given cans to take home and their reactions were assessed. Secondly, taste tests were carried out to see if consumers could tell the difference between Draught Guinness and the canned version. Finally, a simulated market test was carried out. This involved consumers completing a detailed questionnaire after which they were exposed to a reel of advertising before entering a simulated shop. Once inside this shop, consumers were offered a 30 per cent discount on a beer of their choice. Those who chose to purchase Canned Draught Guinness were recontacted later and questioned on their reaction to the product and the likelihood of them purchasing it again.

The results of this extensive research proved extremely encouraging. Perhaps the only stumbling block was the fact that consumers found it hard to believe that real Draught Guinness could truly be poured from a can until they had tried it for themselves. (One of the advertising slogans we used was 'Hard to believe, easy to swallow'.) Once this credibility gap was overcome, and consumers had been persuaded to try the product, repeat purchase levels proved to be excellent.

These steps led in turn to the development of a major advertising campaign – 'Unbelievable but True' – which was

Illustration 2.8
> The advertising slogan 'Hard to Believe, Easy to Swallow' was developed to
> encourage consumers to try out the canned product.

launched in the test market areas of the Midlands, Lancashire
and Yorkshire in April 1988. By the end of that year it was
clear that Canned Draught Guinness was a success and the
new product was launched nationally in March 1989.

Canned Draught Guinness has since been hailed as the
most successful take-home launch of the 1980s and has
underlined Guinness' commitment to innovation. By the
middle of 1991, it was the seventh largest beer brand in a
market where lager accounts for over half of all sales.

Since the mid-1980s, Guinness has concentrated enormous
effort on the marketing of its brands. Through new
distribution agreements, in which joint ventures have played
a significant part, the management of Guinness' extensive
portfolio of brands has been brought back under the control
of the company. Brand extensions, such as Tanqueray
Sterling Vodka in the USA and Johnnie Walker Gold, Oldest
and Premier in the Far East, and technological innovations
such as the development of Draught Guinness in a can have
helped both to create new brand power and to enhance
existing brand strengths.

THE MANAGEMENT OF GLOBAL BRANDS

3

Camillo Pagano
Former Executive Vice President
NESTLÉ SA

In discussing the management of global brands, I would like to start by dismissing some buzz words, including globalisation, regionalisation, macro-markets and micro-markets. These obscure the real issues by creating a cosy sense of over-simplification. They are part of a search for infallible solutions which – fortunately, in my opinion – do not exist in the ever-changing reality of business.

Global Marketing

If global marketing is taken to mean conducting business activities around the world, Nestlé, with a domestic market of less than 3 per cent, has thrived for over a century on global marketing. If global marketing also means global approaches to communication and advertising, then Nestlé is not an example. It owes its growth to highly decentralised operations and the ability to adapt to local conditions, habits and tastes. We believe that in food marketing the closer we are to understanding our consumers, the way they live, eat and make their choices, the more successful we will be.

Because of the diversity of consumer habits with regard to food in markets around the world, the food industry is the least 'globalisable' of businesses. Providing a convenient,

53

Illustration 3.1
The Kit Kat brand was first launched in 1935 by Rowntree and within two years was the company's best seller. This famous snack product and the 'Have a Break, Have a Kit Kat' slogan have become extremely well established in the British market.

quality answer to the entrenched eating habits of consumers requires great flexibility and the capacity to respond to local market requirements. At the same time, persuading consumers to adopt new eating habits, particularly in response to actual and anticipated changes in lifestyle, offers excellent potential for global marketing in the widest sense. In both approaches it is important to consider both cost-effectiveness and the likely success of any innovations.

The only marketing assets which have genuine global application are:

(i) big brands
(ii) underlying attributes of quality, convenience and satisfaction which, in the long run, make big brands.

The gradual changes which are occurring in the market place indicate how industry thinking develops; once in a while, however, it is important to step back to take stock of precisely what has changed and why. And when one does so,

Illustration 3.2
The Milo brand is a powerful product brand within the Nestlé portfolio. The illustration here shows how the strong visual equities of the brand are retained across different languages and cultures.

it is clear that some of the recent changes in the developed world are truly impressive.

Today, we all trade in an environment which is fundamentally different from that of the 1960s, yet some businesses are still using the marketing approaches of thirty years ago. Sadly, even some business schools turn out MBAs who have been taught to use approaches based on case histories that are simply no longer relevant to the realities of the current climate. In the food industry, we need to assess continually the correctness of our overall marketing strategy. If we fail to do so, we shall not benefit from the lessons learnt over the last thirty years.

The table below summarises some of the more important changes that have taken place in marketing over the last thirty to forty years (Figure 3.1). The overwhelmingly important trend has been a switch away from a manufacturing focus towards a far more consumer-oriented approach.

Figure 3.1   Summary of the changes in the marketing environment

50s – 70s		80s – 90s
Large technological differences	◆	Few technological differences
High consumer demand	◆	High manufacturer's offer
Large product volumes	◆	Trend to segmentation
Strong growth of markets	◆	Stagnating total markets
Moderate competitive pressure	◆	Aggressive competition
No trade concentration	◆	Strong trade concentration
Mass consumers	◆	'I am me' consumer
The rational role of advertising: 'Inform and convince'	◆	The emotional role of advertising: 'Seduce and understand me'
Simple media structures	◆	Proliferation of media
Concentration in media usage	◆	Explosion in media usage
Manufacturers decided what consumers should buy	◆	The consumer chooses what he wants
Manufacturer's market	◆	**Consumer market**

Companies who have yet to recognise this fundamental shift in approach will be lucky to survive.

But let us now return to the specifics of the food industry and examine the major issues that confront the industry as we enter the last few years of the twentieth century.

Major Issues

The major problems faced by the food industry and, indeed, many others are:

(i)   How can we convince today's consumer to choose our products instead of our competitors' if there is little or no intrinsic difference between the products in question?

(ii)   How can we identify and efficiently reach those consumers who do have a genuine interest in our various products? The expansion of product choice has created a phenomenon whereby consumers are becoming increasingly indifferent to new product offerings.

(iii) How can we balance the need for a greater success rate and quicker return on investment with the increasing need for product renovation and innovation?

(iv)   How can we get smaller volume products on the shelves and maintain them without having to pay heavy 'extra' allowances to the trade?

(v)   How can we communicate more efficiently and beat media inflation? Traditional media advertising costs are rising at a rate far exceeding national inflation rates. The sheer volume of media advertising tends to increase the costs further, since the message has to be seen more often to create any impact. In addition, we are forced to use many more media outlets to reach the same audience levels we used to reach, for example, with one TV station thirty years ago. And prices for individual TV stations or magazines have not gone down!

Besides these key questions there are other difficult questions which must be faced by brand owners, such as how to keep the balance between immediate sales volumes and long-term brand building needs. Clearly, the answers to such questions vary from industry to industry and even from company to company. All these issues, however, compel us to focus on the central issue of marketing: understanding and managing the power of our brands.

Understanding Brands

There are two kinds of brands today: established brands and new brands. The first make up 90 per cent of the market and most are at least twenty years old. The positive imagery associated with a power brand must be thoroughly understood if its power is to be exploited in building a bigger family of products, or if it is to be extended into new categories.

A contract exists between a brand and its users, especially its heavy users. It is the job of marketing people to strengthen this bond – never to dilute it or to cause uncertainty or frustration – and constantly to build brand authority by keeping the brand relevant and contemporary in a changing world.

The brand authority – that is, what the consumer believes a brand is good at – is the generator of brand power and it drives both the recognition and the reputation of the brand. Brand authority is what makes it so difficult for a new product to penetrate the market; as in politics, unseating the incumbent is a rare event. This is why it makes such sound financial sense for established brands to extend their products across categories and also, in certain cases, for companies to acquire established brands rather than to try to grow a new brand from scratch.

The authoritative brand must reflect the culture of the company that makes it, the culture of the product category it belongs to, and the culture of the countries in which it is sold and should be managed from three perspectives:

  (i)   What it has stood for in the past
 (ii)   What is needed from it today
(iii)   What is expected from it tomorrow

Neglecting the first removes the capacity to build on the past; neglecting the second ignores reality; neglecting the third fails to build for the future.

A consumer above all else buys a product to fill a need or urge. But the brand – the focal point of trust, quality and competence – will determine the consumer's choice. The more a brand is related to a specific product, the more the consumer will match the product's characteristics – taste, feel, touch and experience – with the brand itself. This gives added value to the product and an emotional attachment built around the brand image, both of which provide a solid defence against the competition. Within Nestlé we call specific products enriched with a strong emotional attachment and brand image *product brands.*

Illustration 3.3

The Nesquik range of products benefits from a strong corporate endorsement. This illustration demonstrates quite clearly the interaction of corporate brand and product brand on Nesquik packaging.

But a brand may also be closely associated with a corporate name and encompass much more in product terms than just one product. Here, it may still maintain its empathy and strength but will be credited by the consumer with a more generalised overall competence. We in Nestlé call this a *corporate brand* while other companies use terms such as *umbrella brands* or *pillar brands*. The image of a corporate brand is usually closely identified with what the consumer expects from a manufacturer: trust, a guarantee of quality and know-how in a well defined area. If product brands are linked to a strong corporate brand they will profit from the corporate brand's powerful image and endorsement yet maintain their own individuality. And the product brand will in turn add credibility to the corporate brand image.

The Corporate Brand Concept

Nestlé has always believed in the power of corporate brands and the Maggi brand provides an excellent example of how we use such brands. Historically the Maggi brand was strongly associated with meat bouillons and seasoning products but, as convenience and taste were the recognised added values of the Maggi brand, it has been able to enlarge its product area from bouillons through to soups, sauces and ready-to-eat microwaveable meals. The result is that Maggi is still as young today as it was 100 years ago, and its magic still gives consumers innovative products and ideas. Today's Maggi consumer doesn't just buy one Maggi product but a whole range of products, and is very keen to try any new product on offer from Maggi.

There are however dangers involved in a corporate brand over-extending its competence into too many non-related areas. It may lose its credibility and start to become a mere label without any distinctive features, characteristics or competences. By becoming too much of a catch-all it opens

Illustration 3.4
Originally the Maggi brand was associated with meat bouillon cubes and seasoning products. . . .

Illustration 3.5

. . . .but the brand has successfully extended its core brand equities of taste and convenience to embrace other products such as sauces, soups and ready-to-eat meals.

itself up to attack from focused, specialist competitive brands. Great skill is required to increase the breadth and scope of a corporate brand whilst ensuring that no harm is done to the brand's personality in the process.

Every food manufacturer needs both product brands *and* corporate brands – the former give extra dimension, value and individuality to the products while the latter supply the trust, quality expectations and guarantee. And since the corporate brand is in effect the sum of its parts there must be an ongoing dialogue between the corporate brand and the product brands and never a conflict of interests.

In corporate brand marketing, products and their positionings should be managed in relation to the corporate brand and its area of competence. The corporate brand is based on the tradition of its core products as well as the composite of all its current product brand images. This means that the corporate brand positioning must complement that of its product brands. The relationship of product brands to their corporate brand needs to be carefully monitored according to the 'corporate brand concept'. The consumer needs a clear sense of what the corporate brand stands for and, within that context, a clear view of the sub-positionings of the product brands.

This should not however lead to the corporate brand becoming, in advertising and communications terms, a somewhat abstract and distanced endorsement. Rather, the corporate brand concept should provide a framework within which products – both existing and new – can be fitted profitably. Each addition should bring credibility and strength to the corporate brand.

Managing Corporate Brands

Corporate brand management should be the responsibility of highly experienced, talented individuals. These individuals must assess the value of the product brands against the corporate brand, balancing spending between the two, and they must focus their efforts and expenditure on those product brands whose success will also benefit the corporate brand. They may need courage to refrain from supporting every single product brand, particularly when the corporate brand franchise is sufficiently powerful to carry those products through the trade into the consumer's hands and hence support for all the brands in the portfolio may be unnecessary. For example, the Chambourcy brand in France covers more than forty product brands yet only eight have a separate advertising budget.

The responsibility for corporate branding may also involve sacrifice; in defining the corporate brand positioning one inevitably defines the brand's 'territory' and this necessarily means sacrificing what is outside that territory.

At Nestlé, the guardians of Nestlé's corporate brands and of their respective strategic positionings are the Strategic Business Unit managers. They have long-term strategic responsibility for the coherence, development and territorial efficiency of Nestlé's brands. Their task is to maintain and increase the competitiveness of Nestlé's national operating companies in domestic markets and, in order to enhance their chances of success, the parent company's framework policies on brands and their respective positionings allow for a degree of local adaptation and flexibility. Indeed, there is no single fixed system or structure within Nestlé. In our type of business each brand's positioning and market environment dictates its *modus operandi*.

Buitoni is a good example of the flexibility of approach needed in long-term brand building. Buitoni is managed by a Central Business Unit and as the brand positioning is one of 'authentically Italian', all product recipes are defined and authenticated by an Italian panel. In this instance no country is allowed to adapt the recipes to local taste; if they wish to do this they can introduce the new recipes under either the Maggi or the Findus brands but not under Buitoni. The communication process follows the same principle: all

Illustration 3.6

Buitoni represents the ultimate in authentic Italian cuisine. All recipes are strictly controlled to ensure that they are true to the original Italian recipe – local adaptation of the recipes is forbidden.

advertising is either developed through the Buitoni Business Unit or locally, but local advertising must be cleared by the Central Unit. Such an approach contrasts sharply with the different local positionings of Nestlé's Nescafé soluble coffee brand. These vary from country-to-country according to historical differences in local 'coffee culture'. Thus the Buitoni concept is origin-driven, while the Nescafé concept is culturally-driven.

Nestlé is a company which believes in the power of its brands. We know that as soon as the consumer becomes loyal to one of our brands, in effect we no longer own that brand as it then 'belongs' to the consumer. This attitude has made the Nestlé Company the largest food company in the world and the company's solidity and growth allows Nestlé to stand back frequently and take a look at its business and at the marketing environment. We make a point of listening to the trade and to consumers and we then let common-sense dictate how we adapt ourselves and evolve. Flexibility is the key to our success.

Illustration 3.7

Nescafé is one of the world's great power brands. It pioneered the instant coffee sector of the drinks market and has dominated the market ever since its launch in 1938. Individual brand positionings for Nescafé vary from country to country to take into account differences in 'coffee culture'.

THE IMPORTANCE OF MARKET-PERCEIVED QUALITY

4

Dr Bradley Gale
Founder
MARKET DRIVEN QUALITY INC

Power brands are worth billions of dollars for one reason: they mean quality to the consumer. And this in turn means consumer loyalty, repeat purchases, and word-of-mouth advertising.

Careful research over the past twenty-five years has shown that **the brands that achieve superior profitability are those that have convinced customers they offer superior quality**.

As Figure 4.1 shows, customer perception of quality correlates closely with profit margins. Brands with superior quality earn net margins that are nearly four times as high as those perceived to be inferior. In fact, as we shall see, quality is a more fundamental driver of competitive position and business results than any of the other factors (market share, position on the 'learning curve', low costs, growth of the served market) put forth by strategy gurus.

These statistics are from the Profit Impact of Market Strategy (PIMS) database[1], developed at the Marketing Science Institute and the Strategic Planning Institute in Cambridge, Mass., during the 1970s and 1980s. This database today contains data from some 3000 business units of some 450 companies. The PIMS database is widely recognised as

65

Figure 4.1 Market-perceived quality boosts margins

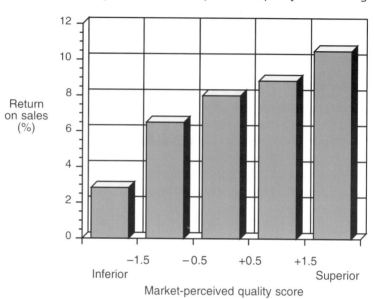

the only complete database in the world of strategy information on many different industries (see box). Moreover, more than 800 of the business units in the PIMS database are consumer businesses that must manage brands. Their performance can be readily compared to judge the value of alternative brand strategies.

Studies on the PIMS database dramatically confirm what the best business people have always known: that customers rely on brands because they want to buy the best possible products, and the enormous profits that owners of successful brands receive are in fact the reward for delivering high quality.

The Wrong Way and the Right Way to Create Brand Power

For many years the majority of managers – and the majority of management experts – ignored the central importance of quality, except in Japan. Many still neglect it today. They cut

The PIMS Database

The Profit Impact of Market Strategy (PIMS) database was created in 1972 at the Marketing Sciences Institute in Cambridge, Mass. Companies who participate in the PIMS programme – some 450 to date – contribute confidential financial, market, customer, and quality information on their lines of business. The database stores information on each of 3000 plus strategic business units without identifying them by name. Thus, researchers can study correlations and trends without violating the confidentiality of the participating organisations.

The PIMS database is widely recognised as the only complete database in the world providing strategic information on a wide variety of industries. A number of different databases can be used to study the effects on sales of changes in such strategic variables as, for example, advertising expenditure, automation or manufacturing costs. Estimates of sales are readily available for a wide variety of companies from a wide variety of sources. But the PIMS database is the only source that enables the analysis of the relationships between key variables and the profits and cash flows of individual strategic business units.

The PIMS database is now maintained by the Strategic Planning Institute, an independent Cambridge-based membership organisation of which Dr Gale was formerly President.

costs in ways that reduce quality. They over-emphasise short-term stratagems such as price promotions, producing quick sales gains but ultimately undermining the customer's perception of quality. Short-term sales gains are measurable, and managers think that market-perceived quality is not. But managers destroy brands when they fail to recognise that **brand power is essentially the power of customer-perceived quality**.

The sad story of Schlitz Brewing illustrates not only the failure of a cheapened product but also the failure of management analysts to understand what brand power is all about. A cost-cutting campaign by managers at Schlitz, the second largest brewer of beer in the United States, reduced the quality of their brew in the early 1970s. Schlitz executives substituted corn syrup and hop pellets for traditional ingredients and shortened the brewing cycle by 50 per cent and then bragged to analysts and other managers about the shortcuts they had taken.

Rather than warning about the likelihood of long-term slippage in brand power and market share, experts congratulated Schlitz for its hard-headedness when in 1973 it achieved higher returns on sales and assets than Anheuser-Busch, the brewer of the number one brand, Budweiser. 'Does it pay to build quality into a product if most consumers don't notice?', asked Forbes.[2] 'Schlitz seems to have a more successful answer than Anheuser.'

Our research shows, however, that consumers consistently recognise inferior products, and the ensuing loss of market share outweighs any saving that managers may have achieved through cost-cutting. In the long run, the beer market proved to be no exception. After initial profit increases in 1973, Schlitz's volume and profits fell rapidly. Schlitz sales had declined 40 per cent by 1980 and the sales ranking of the Schlitz brand had fallen from number two to number seven. Not surprisingly, the Schlitz stock price collapsed from $69 to $5 before the company was bought out by another brewer.

Let us now consider how the best entrepreneurs and managers create power brands. The basic mechanism is laid out in Figure 4.2. They start with a clear sense of the needs and desires of a well-defined group of customers. They produce products and supply the associated services that meet those needs exceptionally well. Effective 'quality control' measures ensure they 'do things right the first time' in delivering those products and services. Therefore, they achieve superior quality in areas that matter to the customer together with a cost structure no higher than that of lower-quality competitors. Then, they advertise to communicate their products' advantages. The customer perceives the quality and the exceptional value offered. The result: a power brand is created and dominant market share follows.

Figure 4.2 Power brands: the essentials

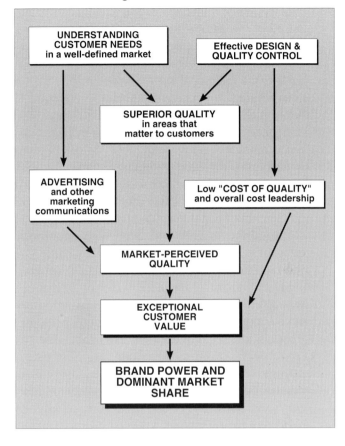

The mechanism seems simple. But how many businesses are able to navigate their way through changing market conditions? In fact, how many are really trying?

Market-Perceived Quality is Measurable

Market-perceived quality is as measureable as market share, and should form the heart of any brand strategy. Consider, for instance, the case of Perdue Farms, which has in the last twenty years become *the* power brand for uncooked chicken on the eastern seaboard of the United States.

Because the data in the PIMS database comes directly from participating companies, individual companies' stories must be kept confidential. But other sources provide concrete examples that support the statistical inferences we draw from the database. In the early 1980s I spoke at a meeting of the Southeast Egg & Poultry Association, a group of Perdue's competitors and people who have watched Perdue's success with considerable interest. I had a chance to ask them to compare Perdue's chicken with their own. The result demonstrates why and how Frank Perdue has become synonymous in consumers' minds with excellence.

Many of the members of the Southeast Egg & Poultry Association remembered the days before Perdue inherited his chicken business from his father. In that era, chickens were a commodity, as they had been for generations. The customer generally ignored the brand names some companies put on their chickens and bought principally on price.

Frank Perdue started his work by learning what customers wanted in their chickens and then learning how to deliver it. I asked a panel of members of the Southeast Egg & Poultry Association to tell me the key characteristics that affected customers' buying decisions and to estimate customers' ratings of the quality of Perdue chickens on those factors versus customers' ratings of average chickens (that is, the chickens sold by other members of the association). The results, with ratings on a scale of 1 to 10, appear in Figure 4.3.

Frank Perdue's competitors recognised that his product was superior to ordinary chickens on almost every non-price attribute. This success was not surprising; Perdue had started his efforts to create his brand with research to learn just what consumers wanted in their chickens. Then he had invested in careful breeding and improved feed to give customers what his surveys showed they wanted: meatier, yellower chickens. He even purchased a turbine engine to blow-dry his chickens thoroughly, just before they reached the torching station where their pinfeathers were supposed to be burned off. Though a few pinfeathers still slip through, they are less common on Perdue chickens than on those of competitors.

Note that quality as Perdue provided it is not quality as the 'quality departments' of organisations normally define it.

Figure 4.3 Chicken business: customer's purchase decision

Key purchase criteria*	Relative importance weights: (sum to 1.00)	Performance ratings: 1 to 10 (10 = best) Perdue	Others	Rating Difference	Weighted Rating Difference
	(a)	(b)	(c)	(d = b − c)	(e = a × d)
Product:					
Yellow bird	.10	8.1	7.2	+0.9	+0.09
Meat-to-bone	.20	9.0	7.3	+1.7	+0.34
No pinfeathers	.20	9.2	6.5	+2.7	+0.54
Fresh	.15	8.0	8.0	0.0	0.00
Service:					
Availability	.10	8.0	8.0	0.0	0.00
Brand image	.25	9.4	6.4	+3.0	+0.75
Sum of weights:	1.00				
Weighted score		8.80	7.08	+1.72	
Perdue's Market Perceived Quality score					+1.72

*Criteria inculde all the non-price factors that count in the purchase decision

Customer value is 'the quality you get for the price that you pay'

Elements of customer value	Before	After
Perdue's market perceived quality		
Image	commodity	superior
Score	0.00	1.72
Perdue's price versus others	same	premium
Weight place on:		
Market perceived quality	10	70
Price	90	30

Many organisations still think of 'quality' as conformance to some internally defined 'requirements' or specifications. And of course achieving excellent conformance quality is vitally important: close conformance to specifications is often crucial to giving the customer what he or she wants, and it also leads to lower costs by reducing re-work, customer complaint-handling time, and the confusion that unpredictable performance brings to an organisation. But conformance quality is only a portion of what quality means to the consumer. Frank Perdue succeeded because he listened to how *the customer* defined quality. He provided what the consumer wanted and he made sure the consumer had a chance to learn about and remember his quality improvements.

Perdue moved from the price promotion that dominated the chicken business to carefully thought-out advertising produced by the firm Scali McCabe. 'Buy Perdue chickens – You get an extra bite in every breast', said thousands of commercials. The result of surveys, operational improvements and advertising has been that Frank Perdue's brand has achieved quality and market-share leadership.

The right-hand column of Figure 4.3 shows how a 'perceived quality score' for Perdue relative to the rest of the industry can be calculated. For each attribute, the estimated relative weight in the customer's decision (provided, in this case, by the panel from the Southeast Egg & Poultry Association) is multiplied by the rating difference for Perdue chickens versus those produced by others. This indicates how Perdue's score in each rating category influences the consumer's overall decision. The calculation shows that Perdue has a perceived quality score of +1.72 relative to others in Perdue's industry. (The highest possible relative perceived quality score – if your product were perfect in every way and the competitor's product earned a 1 on all attributes – would be +9; the lowest would be –9.) The market-perceived quality score relative to competition is a more important measure than the statistics that companies traditionally track, such as the percentage of consumers who report themselves 'satisfied' in surveys. The 'percent satisfied' may change very slowly when another competitor introduces a better product. But the market-perceived quality score will change immediately.

A score of +1.72 represents a very substantial difference – on a measure that is more meaningful than any measure of conformance quality. It means Perdue can charge a premium for his chickens and competitors have to sell theirs at a discount relative to his. Naturally, Perdue earns enormous profits. And Perdue achieved all this because he made decisions that most management systems – even the management systems in companies that are today managing some of the world's most powerful brands – would reject. When he bought the turbine engine to blow-dry his chickens better and eliminate pinfeathers, he was making a capital investment that neither expanded capacity nor cut costs. He was simply responding to what his surveys told him customers wanted; he was making an investment in brand power. He had no quantitative analysis of the benefits at all. In most companies, the capital appropriation system rejects such proposals. Why does Perdue invest this way when others do not? Because of Perdue's deep commitment to market-perceived quality.

Understanding Consumer Decision-Making

Customers make purchase decisions based on their perceptions of **value**: that is, of quality relative to price. Quality includes all the non-price attributes that count in the purchase decision, both attributes of the product itself and attributes of the associated consumer service (Figure 4.4). When organisations provide less perceived value than their competitors, as, for example, USA automakers did in the 1980s relative to the Japanese, they lose market share.

Customers, however, will not act on the value you provide unless you help them to perceive it, and many managers fail to do that. For instance, in the United States from 1977 to 1987, the percentage of marketing budgets spent on advertis-

Figure 4.4   Model of brand selection

- Customer buys on value
- Value equals quality relative to price
- Quality includes all non-price attributes that count in the purchase decision
  - Product
  - Customer service
- Quality, price and value, are not absolute, but relative to competitors

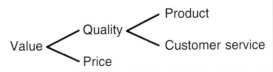

ing (as opposed to promotions such as cents-off coupons) fell from 60 per cent to 40 per cent, according to studies by Donnelly Marketing. Advertising encourages customers to recognise the quality you offer. Sales promotions, if they affect your customer's perception of your quality at all, tend to cheapen your image. But price promotions often produce short-term sales increases, so many managers over-emphasise them.

The PIMS database shows that the long-run result of that is likely to be a decline in both perceived quality and profitability. Advertising plays a key driving function in helping companies become perceived-quality leaders. Studies on the PIMS database show that there is a strong positive correlation between spending a larger portion of the sales dollar on advertising and achieving higher perceived quality (Figure 4.5). (The perceived quality scores in all exhibits were calculated using a methodology similar to that described in the Perdue example above.)

Improvements in perceived quality in turn lead to high market share (Figure 4.6) and market leaders spend to build

Figure 4.5 Superior quality and heftier advertising go together

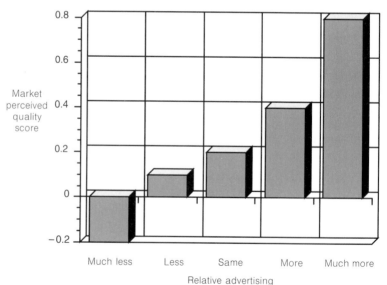

Figure 4.6 Improving quality boosts market share

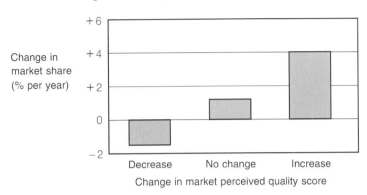

Change in market share (% per year)

Change in market perceived quality score

Figure 4.7 Market leaders spend to build the franchise

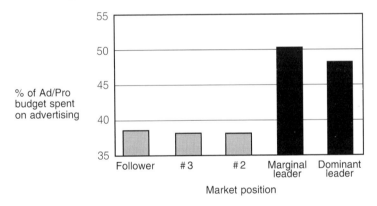

% of Ad/Pro budget spent on advertising

Market position

the franchise (Figure 4.7). Both superior perceived quality *and* heftier advertising each seem independently to help companies to achieve price premiums (Figure 4.8).

The result is that companies that spend a larger share of their sales income on advertising tend to be much more profitable than companies that spend less. Brands that spend a much larger than average share of their sales on advertising earn an average return-on-investment of 32 per cent while brands that advertise much less than their competitors average only 17 per cent.

It is difficult to judge just how much of this advantage is due to advertising itself. To some extent, companies with

Figure 4.8 Superior quality and heftier advertising yield price premiums

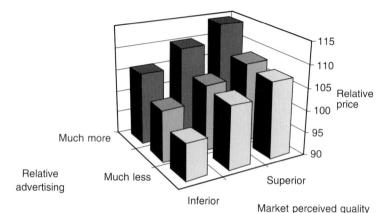

high quality simply have more to say in their advertising, so they are more likely to spend money saying it. We can, however, measure the impact of advertising more directly by looking at how advertising affects market share over time. When we do, we find there is strong evidence that companies with high-quality products can often increase their profitability by increasing their advertising spending.

In one study, for instance, we looked at 314 fast-moving consumer goods businesses over a four-year period. We examined how changes in market share were correlated with changes in spending on media advertising, changes in spending on sales promotions, changes in spending on the company sales force, new product introductions, relative quality improvements, the growth of the served market, and other factors.

We found that increases in advertising expenditures were closely correlated with gains in market share *even after adjusting for the effects of all other factors*. In contrast, increased use of cents-off coupons, special price breaks and other sales promotion showed no statistically significant correlation with market share changes over the four-year period at all.

Another study developed even more evidence that, as long as you have a top three brand, advertising benefits a business more than sales promotions. We divided the fast-moving consumer goods businesses in the PIMS database into three

Figure 4.9 Profitability, market rank and the advertising/promotion mix

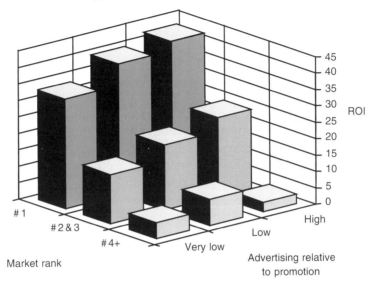

groups: those that spent a significantly larger than average percentage of their marketing budget on promotions (average promotional spending for this group was 77 per cent of the marketing budget), those that split their budgets more-or-less evenly between advertising and promotions, and those that spent the bulk of their budgets (an average of 66 per cent) on advertising. We found that the average return on investment for the promotionally oriented businesses was 18.1 per cent. The average for the mixed businesses was 27.3 per cent, and the average for the advertising-oriented businesses was 30.5 per cent (Figure 4.9). Note, however, that for brands ranked number four or worse, profitability actually decreases from the low to the high in the 'Advertising relative to Promotion' category.

Quality and Market Share

The first conclusions of market strategy research in the late 1960s and early 1970s emphasised the importance of market share more than quality. It was not until the late 1970s, when we developed better methods of estimating customer-perceived quality, that the paramount importance of quality to profitability became clear.

Managers of branded products still need to understand the close relationship between market share and profitability. High market share businesses, even those with merely average perceived quality, tend to enjoy economies of scale and to achieve better turnover of inventory and receivables; they can also perform more research and development than low-share businesses. Moreover, many consumers prefer to do business with high market share businesses because they perceive less risk in purchasing from a business whose position in the market appears to be secure. Thus, high market share businesses are exceptionally profitable while many low market share businesses are marginal operations.

In fact, at any point in time, the correlation between profitability and market share is slightly stronger than the correlation between profitability and market-perceived quality. But this kind of 'snapshot' can be misleading. Market-perceived quality is a more important measure of competitiveness than market share for two key reasons:

(i) Firstly, most market leaders first had to develop quality leadership to achieve their large share position. Superior quality is the base upon which market leadership is usually built.

(ii) Secondly, over all the time periods for which we have data, businesses that begin with a large share of the market tend to lose share. By contrast, those that begin with superior quality tend to hold or gain share.

Thus, market share is often a lagging indicator of a company's performance; quality is the clear key to success.

Many business executives feel satisfied by simply tracking their market shares and see little need for other measures. However, they will have a problem if market share starts to slip and stops responding to quick strategic changes such as new packaging or a fresh advertising campaign. They are likely to discover it is too late to halt the downward slide. By contrast, those who also track market-perceived quality (not simply customer satisfaction, but perceived quality relative to competitors) have a leading indicator of what will happen to market share. And, even more importantly, they also have detailed information from the marketplace about key brand selection attributes, importance weights and performance ratings versus competitors to tell them how these elements of customer value are changing and what to do about it – while they can still control their own destiny.

The most effective way to gain market share is simply to provide a product your customers like better than the competition's. Figure 4.10 shows how dominant businesses tend to have superior market-perceived quality scores while follower businesses tend to have inferior scores.

Many market share-oriented strategies are doomed to failure because they fail to create a quality leader. When Frank Lorenzo patched together America's largest airline from mergers that combined Texas Air, Continental, People Express and Eastern, the result was an unwieldy monster. It did achieve some economies of scale, as connections among the parts of the system were arranged to make it easy for

Figure 4.10 Market leadership is based on superior market-perceived quality

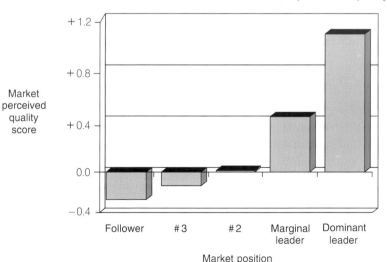

people to board Texas Air-affiliated carriers and take them to any other part of the United States. But the patchwork of different organisational cultures could not deliver the excellence that quality-oriented, culturally consistent airlines like American and Delta achieved. Texas Air's perceived quality score relative to its competitors, had it bothered to calculate it, would have been terrible. Eventually, the entire company fell apart.

On the other hand, even true power brands cannot raise their relative prices forever **unless at the same time they also continually increase their relative perceived quality**. Studies on the PIMS database show that market-leading brands tend to lose market share if they are not quality leaders, even when they do not raise their relative prices. When companies *do* raise their prices without also increasing relative perceived quality, market share can erode dramatically. In the supermarket, where dominant brands raised relative prices dramatically in the 1980s while doing little to improve relative perceived quality, we see that happening; the shares of the top three brands have declined significantly in disposable diapers, salad dressings, baking mixes, household cleaners, popcorn, barbecue sauces, dishwashing detergent and canned cat food.

Figure 4.11 shows that market-perceived quality and market share each appear to contribute dramatically to profitability. In many cases, as we saw in Figure 4.6, market-perceived quality is actually a leading indicator that predicts future market share. Companies too small to become share leaders of large markets often succeed by defining a niche and becoming share leaders there, as Briggs & Stratton does with the lawnmower engine market and Dr Scholl does in foot care.

There may, in fact, exist opportunities to create a power brand even with quality that is merely average. You can create a product to serve a market that has not been served before, for instance, and protect your product with patents. Or if you are an early entrant in a rapidly growing market, aggressive advertising and marketing may help you win a dominant – and highly profitable – position like the position Lotus 1–2–3 won in the computer spreadsheet market.

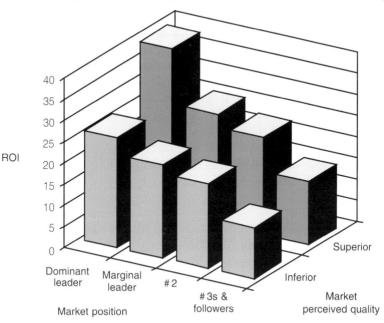

Figure 4.11 Quality and market position drive profitability

The relationship between market share and profitability is very strong in industries that devote an exceptionally large share of costs to R & D and marketing, such as computer software and cosmetics. In manufacturing businesses, the difference in return-on-investment between number one businesses and businesses ranked number five or lower is twelve points. But in R & D and marketing-intensive businesses, the difference between number one businesses and number five or lower businesses is an incredible twenty-six points. Number 1 businesses in such fields earn returns on investment of 36 per cent, number two businesses earn 23 per cent, number three businesses earn 17 per cent, number four businesses earn 16 per cent and number five or lower businesses earn only 10 per cent. Thus market share-oriented strategies, such as advertising heavily to gain an early lead in rapidly expanding niches, are particularly important in such industries.

But if you forget that quality is king – that you succeed in the marketplace because your name is synonymous with excellence to people in your served market – your strategy will ultimately fail.

Real Brand Power

One recent story that illustrates the essence of brand power is the re-invigoration of Gillette, one of the world's most important 'power brands'. Since the nineteenth century Gillette has succeeded because its name has been synonymous with quality. Sponsoring the World Series in the 1950s, the company proudly proclaimed Gillette as the:

'Only Way to Get a Decent Shave'

However, in the early 1970s, Gillette's strength was sapped by diversification into fields where it could not be the quality leader. So competitors attacked its heart; disposable razors offered a 'decent shave' and were sold at less than $2 per half-dozen. Gillette fought back and took a good portion of the disposables market, but the trend cut sharply into sales of $3-and-up shaving systems such as the Trac II and the Atra. That threw the market for blades – the 'continuing tribute to the company' paid by users everywhere – into decline.

Profits margins also slid for the simple reason that consumers no longer perceived quality differences among competitors in the shaving business. Many people, inside and outside Gillette, concluded that razors were inevitably becoming merely a commodity. They concluded the company should sharply cut overhead in its 'cash cow' shaving business and four separate takeover attempts in the 1980s sought to force the company to do exactly that.

But the critics did not understand the real problem, which was that Gillette had lost sight of what its brand was. It was natural that Gillette's margins would tend to decline when it failed to make clear it had products of superior quality. The battle in the marketing of disposables – a significant innovation that naturally would cost Gillette some profits – had caused the company to lose sight of the quality advantages it still possessed. The Trac II and Atra shavers still gave many men a better shave than any disposables but the noise of promotion of Gillette's 'Good News' disposables obscured that fact.

Eventually the company began to practise good brand stewardship again. In 1979 it began development of the new Sensor razor, a process that would take more than a decade. Next, starting in Europe, it refocused its marketing. Leaving its disposables to sell themselves, it began putting all its marketing money into shaving systems that used replaceable cartridges. Thus, the razor-and-blade business began to yield bigger profits and when the Sensor was introduced in 1990, men demonstrated emphatically that the availability of a 'decent shave' at a lower price did not keep them from being willing to spend money for quality. The Sensor's blades float on tiny springs to conform better to the contours of the shaver's face. Protected by seventeen patents, the manufacture of the Sensor blade cartridge demands a machine that can make ninety-three precise laser welds per second. Initial sales exceeded company projections by 30 per cent and might have been even higher if the company had been able to meet the demand.

Though it has abandoned businesses where it could not become the quality leader, Gillette has scored similar successes with its Braun small appliances, Oral-B toothbrushes and PaperMate Flexgrip pens. Its sales and profits are at record levels and some analysts are forecasting 20 per cent-a-year profit increases. These are dramatic gains for a large company whose businesses are all more-or-less mature and easily dismissed as 'commodities'.

The achievement of market-perceived quality seems to produce superior returns in any industry. Marketers can create brand power and superior returns almost anywhere, provided they focus on becoming perceived quality leaders.

Notes

1. A fuller discussion of the PIMS research project and its results appears in Robert D. Buzzell and Bradley T. Gale, *The PIMS Principles* (New York: The Free Press, 1987).
2. *Forbes*, 1974.

ADDING BRAND VALUE 5

Sir Allen Sheppard
Chairman and Group Chief Executive
GRAND METROPOLITAN PLC

Introduction

At Grand Metropolitan we believe our brands to be our most valuable assets. Our businesses in foods, drinks and retailing are all about consumer brands. We use brands to add value to our food and drink products and to our retail outlets, encouraging consumer loyalty and confidence. This in turn allows us to earn enhanced profits which benefits shareholders and staff alike.

Brands are the core of our business. We could, if we so wished, subcontract all the production, distribution, sales and service functions and, provided that we retained ownership of our brands, we would continue to be successful and profitable. It is our brands that provide the profits of today and guarantee the profits of the future.

Our annual marketing expenditure to launch, maintain, build and add value to these brands exceeds £800 million. But even this is only part of the cost since our marketing effort indirectly involves most of our people. These costs must be accounted for through the annual profit and loss account in line with worldwide accounting standards. We take this one step further, however. We believe that the cost of purchased brands, which does not go through the profit and loss account, should also appear on the balance sheet – provided it is below market value. This is in line with the way in which we treat other substantial assets. Each year we verify that the

85

value of those purchased brands is above the cost shown in our balance sheet.

No single wholly satisfactory means of valuing brands yet exists. But a reliable and verifiable conclusion can be drawn if several methods are used together. I review some of these methods later in this chapter. There is, however, a pressing need for the accounting profession to work out a globally acceptable means of brand valuation.

There is, of course, more to brand valuation than accounting standards. Brand valuation techniques can be used to assist brand managers in monitoring the success of their brands. Our brand managers face the challenge of increasing the value of their brands, but how can they tell how well they are doing? And, for that matter, how can senior management ensure that the work of the junior brand manager is actually enhancing brand value rather than the opposite? Most companies rely on short-term, partial measurements such as market share or profitability, but these may distort the long-term picture. As long-term players, we want more satisfactory measures of brand value and equity to become available. A better informed management would be better placed to add maximum value to their brands to the long-term benefit of staff and shareholders. Techniques for measuring and monitoring brand value are therefore of critical importance.

Brands are our Most Valuable Assets

Branding irons were once applied to wooden barrels and the rumps of cattle, identifying both owner and origin. Today, a brand does far more than this. It provides the consumer with a reassurance of quality and consistency. A good brand is easy to remember and it can often command a premium price over its competitors, as well as high and, more importantly, reliable volumes. A commodity can always be duplicated; brands, however, are by their very nature unique. The steady volumes generated by power brands allow economies of scale and permit more effective cost control. The combination of premium price, significant and reliable volume and a low cost base translate into substantial and predictable profits.

Brand owners can exploit the reputation and image of their brands to add value to products or services thus enhancing profits and cash flow. The stronger the ownership, the more secure the future of those profits, so it is sensible for the brand owner to register the trade mark legally wherever it is worthwhile and possible to do so. However, one need not register a trade mark in order to use a brand; registration simply prevents others using it or anything close to it. To draw a parallel with home ownership, legal trade mark ownership proves title and puts a lock on the front door so we all sleep better at night. The brand itself is the asset; the trade mark is only security.

If this view is accepted, it may seem that the accountancy profession, in recognising trade marks as assets while being ambivalent about brands, has its priorities wrong. We should however be clear about the meaning of the word 'asset'. The American accounting definition of an asset comes from the Financial Accounting Standards Board 1980, para 20:[1]

- It involves a probable future benefit that provides a capacity, singly or in combination with other assets, to contribute directly or indirectly to future net cash flows.

- It requires that a particular entity can obtain the benefit and control others' access to it.

- It specifies that the transaction or other event giving rise to the enterprise's right to or control of the benefit must already have occurred.

In short, this definition requires that an asset must be likely to earn money and should be owned by you. Clearly, if we accept this definition there can be very little doubt that a brand is an asset.

In the case of Grand Metropolitan, brands are central to our business, whether they be in drinks, food or retail and our brands add considerable value in the eyes of our consumers. In our annual report and accounts the words 'adding value' appear under our corporate name, together with a hallmark which identifies our key markets and reflects the origins of the branding process. In short, our company is all about brands. We invest in research and development programmes relating to them, we launch them, nurse them, build them and revive them when we have to. Brands are the lifeblood of Grand Met and it is our brands which will provide our shareholders with their dividends this year, next year and for a hundred years to come. Our shareholders have every reason to be proud of Pillsbury, Green Giant, Häagen-Dazs, Burger King, Cinzano (Plate 9), Smirnoff, J&B Rare, Malibu (Plate 10), Piat d'Or, Baileys Irish Cream (Plate 11) and all the others. We feature them in our annual report because we think shareholders would like to know more about them. We are in no doubt that they are our most valuable assets, just as our people are our most precious resource. What is less clear is how that value should be represented on the balance sheet.

Well Balanced Balance Sheets

A balance sheet is supposed to do many, often inconsistent, things. It is supposed to reflect the cost of a company's assets and liabilities rather than their value, except in situations where cost is above market value. While intended primarily for shareholders, balance sheets are also used by creditors, bankers, advisers, tax authorities, joint venture partners, government departments, Stock Markets and a variety of interested parties.

In addition balance sheets contain important information for those people working within the organisation who spend so much of their own time and effort in making the company successful.

In Grand Metropolitan's annual report and accounts the holding company balance sheet and Group consolidated balance sheet each appear on successive pages. These balance sheets are then followed by sixteen pages of accounting policies and explanatory notes. Shareholders, who have invested their own money in the business, are clearly entitled to all this information and, in my experience, always prefer to have more information rather than less.

In addition, balance sheets must provide a 'snap-shot' of the state of a company at a particular point in time (though a company may be in fine financial health at the year end but subsequent events may change the situation radically) and they must also be prepared on a consistent basis from one year to the next – financial analysts rightly place great emphasis on the maintenance of consistent accounting policies. Finally, balance sheets have to cope with differing accounting standards around the world; brands in particular are treated in varying ways, as is their historical antecedent, 'goodwill'.

Grand Met attempts to steer a conservative course through this cat's cradle of conflicting requirements. It owns global brands, trades in all continents and has an international shareholder base. In the last five years Grand Met has also made many successful acquisitions and the acquisitions of Heublein and Pillsbury stand out both in terms of scale as well as the benefits to shareholders. Both these companies own brands of outstanding quality – Heublein has the world's leading vodka brand, Smirnoff, and Pillsbury owns the Pillsbury, Green Giant, Burger King and Häagen Dazs brands among others. Acquiring these power brand portfolios cost a considerable amount of money over and above the net asset value of each company as revealed by their balance sheets.

UK accounting rules currently require that the purchase goodwill arising from an acquisition should be written off against shareholders' funds in the balance sheet, or should be included on the balance sheet and amortised over not more than forty years. Had Grand Metropolitan been forced to write off the entire goodwill involved in these two acquisitions, the company's consolidated balance sheet would have shown by September 1989 a net worth of only £190 million against a stockmarket value at that time of £5.9 billion. This absurdity was avoided by taking into account the goodwill relating to the value of the brands and including this value on the balance sheet. The value of the brands owned by the Heublein and Pillsbury companies was estimated to amount to some £2.3 billion and the group's net assets, as restated, therefore amounted to some £2.5 billion. Our approach to balance sheet accounting for intangibles met with the approval of our auditors who gave our accounts a clean audit opinion. Other illustrious companies such as Guinness, United Biscuits, Cadbury Schweppes and Ladbroke have followed our example and include a value for their acquired brands on their balance sheets.

The UK Statement of Accounting Practice (SSAP23) says:

> Where a business combination is accounted for as an acquisition, the fair value of the purchase consideration should, for the purpose of consolidated financial statements, be allocated between the underlying net tangible *and intangible* assets, other than goodwill, on the basis of the fair value to the acquiring company in accordance with the requirements of SSAP14.

We interpret this as clearly supporting our balance sheet presentation.

In determining our policy, however, we decided to include only those brands acquired since 1 January 1985 in order to minimise debate about their cost. The principal brands accounted for in this way are Smirnoff, Pillsbury, Green Giant and Burger King. We review the valuation annually to calculate whether there has been any permanent decrease in value and since all of these brands are USA-based, they are carried in US dollars. Consequently, there is an annual movement in the brand value as expressed in sterling due to exchange rate fluctuations. We would be disappointed, however, if there was ever any decrease in the dollar value of our brands, given the money and effort we put behind them.

Some countries have accounting standards which require companies to amortise brand values and we believe this to be quite inappropriate. Products have life cycles but brands need not; indeed, their longevity can be remarkable. Many of the brands that were leaders in their categories in 1933 are still leaders today, as Figure 5.1 below demonstrates.

No natural process of decay dictates the life of brands; their longevity or otherwise depends mainly on how well they are managed. Of course, management cannot control all the variables since whole markets can decline, taking their brands with them. But a brand can long outlive the product to which it was originally attached if management actively develops and manages it.

It is important for our shareholders that they know how well the directors understand and apply key branding skills to the benefit of the business. By showing the cost of purchased brands on the balance sheet and accounting for any decrease in value we enable shareholders to see more clearly what most matters to the business and how well the key assets within the business are being managed.

Figure 5.1 Brand leaders in the UK and USA: 1933–93

UK BRANDS			
Brand	Market	1933 Position	Current Position
Hovis	Bread	1	1
Stork	Margarine	1	1
Kellogg's	Cornflakes	1	1
Gillette	Razors	1	1
Schweppes	Mixers	1	1
Colgate	Toothpaste	1	1
Kodak	Film	1	1
Hoover	Vacuum cleaners	1	1

US BRANDS			
Brand	Market	1933 Position	Current Position
Eastman Kodak	Cameras/Film	1	1
Del Monte	Canned Fruit	1	1
Wrigley	Chewing gum	1	1
Nabisco	Biscuits	1	1
Gillette	Razors	1	1
Coca-Cola	Soft drinks	1	1
Campbells	Soup	1	1
Ivory	Soap	1	1
Goodyear	Tyres	1	1

Illustration 5.1
The world's biggest vodka brand, Smirnoff, was acquired by Grand Metropolitan as part of the Heublein acquisition – writing off the goodwill involved in this deal would have depleted our net equity to an absurdly low level.

The US accounting standard for intangibles is interesting (Accounting Principles Board's Opinion No. 17, August 1970):[2]

> The Board concludes that a company should record as assets the costs of intangible assets acquired from other enterprises or individuals. Costs of developing, maintaining or restoring intangible assets, which are not specifically identifiable, have indeterminate lives, or are inherent in a continuing business, should be deducted from income when incurred.

On this basis, a brand must be recorded as an asset if it has a determinate life. Yet as we discussed above, brands can live forever if they are continually refreshed through the launch of new extensions, formulations or variants. In our view a valuable asset that can last in effect forever must be worth more than a similar asset that expires after only five years. It does not therefore seem logical to place depreciating assets on the balance sheet while omitting those which are blessed with longevity.

In pursuit of the properly balanced balance sheet, we did not take the entire difference between the price paid and the valuation of tangible assets as the value of the brands, although there is an argument for doing this – we do not acquire companies for more than they are worth and indeed, in the case of Heublein, there is some evidence we paid less than it was worth. Pillsbury was a hard and long battle and we paid only what the market established. Even so, we chose to make some independent calculations of brand values to give conservative figures within this overall goodwill limit. In practice, we attributed £1.8 billion to brands and wrote off goodwill of about £1.3 billion. The resulting figure is described as 'cost' but is substantiated by the valuation exercises to verify that it is indeed a 'fair value at acquisition'.

We believe that accounting practice will increasingly recognise the need to include brands on the balance sheet at acquired cost or market value, whichever is the lower. The debate will ultimately produce a better working practice and generally accepted standards will emerge. These need however to be global, just as our brands are global, and shareholders need to be informed as to what these standards are. In short, we need universal standards for properly-balanced balance sheets and Grand Met will do all it can to bring this about.

Valuation Methods

Physicists have long struggled with the common view that what you cannot see either does not exist or will not do so for long. In reality, however, business intangibles may be less subject to decay and obsolescence than other more tangible assets. In response to this we, in common with most companies, now capitalise significant computer software developments while we write off hardware more rapidly than we might have done a few years ago.

Conventionally, there are two stages in brand valuation. The first is to calculate the after-tax profit or cash flow attributable to the brand, the second is to roll this up in some way into a capital sum. In practice these two stages may be intertwined as one affects the other. The three main methods of establishing the annual benefit brought to brand owners by their brands are:

  (i)   Premium earnings
 (ii)   Equivalent (or notional) royalties
(iii)   Brand earnings/alternative return on assets.

The premium earnings approach focuses on the difference between brand and the equivalent non-branded cash flows. This is not just a question of price but should also extend to volume, the steadiness of volume and resulting cost savings. Many assumptions have to be made and it is often difficult to establish the price premium of some brands. Not everything is as obvious as the difference between the price of Smirnoff and that of other lesser vodkas on the same shelf. Moreover, in the case of large, fast-moving brands premium earnings may be enhanced by volume and the reliability of that volume and this too needs to be taken into account. Green Giant is a case in point.

Notional royalties, the second main method used, have the advantage of simplicity. In the case of the Smirnoff brand, our drinks division, International Distillers and Vintners, had been paying royalties to Heublein before our acquisition of that company. As those royalties had been recently negotiated at arms length we had immediate access to relevant market data and could have used the notional royalty method of valuation quite readily. In practice, however, this approach is likely to be of declining use for two reasons: first, as major companies become global they are less willing to license third parties, so the data upon which to base such royalties will become scarcer; and secondly, many countries are resisting royalty-type agreements for exchange control reasons and tax reasons. However, this remains a valuable approach for the immediate future.

The third method of establishing the annual benefit of a brand relates to 'Brand earnings/alternative return on assets'. Here the cash flow must be isolated from the brand and then separated from the generic equivalent. That in turn is calculated as the opportunity rate of return on the capital (that is, the assets excluding the brand itself) employed in producing the product. The remainder is the cash flow that can be attributed to the brand asset.

In all instances, however, once the annual benefit has been established, valuation is relatively straightforward. One can either discount the future cash flows or apply an earnings multiplier to average historic cash flows or to the first year estimated figure. We in fact do both.

We are also well aware that discounted cash flows are sensitive to interest and growth rates and terminal values, though one should look at such projections to establish their credibility; also that earnings multipliers can be found in the marketplace as companies and brands change hands, so this method is the one which is most familiar to investors, corporate finance people and analysts.

There is another school of thought, one where Interbrand are the leading exponents, that the marketplace multiples are inadequate or too rarely available to be used as benchmarks so it is better to create a theoretical model and assign multiples to brand cash flows according to an analysis of relative brand strength. The Interbrand method for calculating brand strength is made up of seven key factors:

   (i)   Leadership
  (ii)   Brand stability
 (iii)   Market stability
 (iv)   Internationality
  (v)   Trend
 (vi)   Marketing support
(vii)   Protection (trade mark security)

The brand is assessed on each of these factors and an overall brand strength score is calculated; it is this which determines the discount rates which are applied to future brand cash flows, or the multiples which are applied to current brand cash flows. Whether or not one agrees with their approach, it is gratifying that in their recent book (*Brands : An International Review* by Interbrand, 1990) they rate our brands Baileys Irish Cream, Smirnoff and Green Giant (Plate 12) so highly.[3]

Interbrand's approach is not in fact very far removed from our own internal accounting policy which has been agreed with our auditors:

A brand should only be valued if its name/trade mark is protected by law or other similar means in at least its major markets. Provided this is the case, the brand strength and hence an appropriate multiple should be decided by considering the following factors, ranked broadly in order of importance:

— the position of the brand in its market
— the position of competitors in the market
— the financial strength and commitment of the competition
— the diversity of the products covered by the brand
— the volatility of the market
— the degree of technological change associated with the products
— the level of public awareness of the brand
— the level of recent marketing support for the brand (to indicate any potential future downturn in demand)
— the impact of Government and other regulatory and pressure groups on the brand
— the internationality of the brand.

Chris Macrae[4] proposes an alternative analysis and classification system as follows:

Figure 5.2   World class brand classification system

Column 1:	Column 2:	Column 3:
Is brand world class?	Is the brand expandable?	Does brand have defendable marketing edge?
A = Global	A = Above average	A = Pre-emptive
B = International with limits to expansion	B = Average	B = Average
	C = Below average	C = Below Average
C = Local		

He rates Disney, Hilton, Sony, Lacoste and Benetton as brands AAA, while he views BCB and BCC brands as being difficult for multinational corporations to manage. He goes on to pay tribute to our success with the J&B Rare (Plate 13) brand but he does not give it a rating and nor, unlike Interbrand, does he translate the classification system into valuation multiples.

Finally, I reproduce in Figure 5.3 a review of the principles of brand valuation, to which I am indebted to Peter Farquhar, Julia Han and Yuji Ijiri.[5]

Figure 5.3 Principles of brand valuation

(1) **Define that which is to be evaluated**

Key questions for the valuation analysis are (a) what exactly is the brand? (b) what is the target market? (c) what are the intended uses of the brand? (d) what is the context of ownership of the brand?

(2) **Establish the value premise**

The basis for value might be incremental profitability, total value, discounted cash flow, royalty rate, income momentum, or some other measure.

(3) **Separate the brand from other sources of value**

The brand's value can be intertwined both with the tangible product and related physical resources and with other intangible assets, such as human resources, know-how, company image and so forth.

(4) **Forecast the brand's future uses and value**

A brand's value depends not only on its existing uses but also on a forecast of possible extensions, portfolio effects, new markets, licensing activities and other future uses. This forecast should make explicit assumptions about the level of future marketing support and ownership.

(5) **Assure reliability of the brand valuation**

The subjective judgements used in brand valuation must be consistent across different individuals, assets, companies and time.

(6) **Check for validity and auditability**

The brand valuation method must provide both checks on the validity of its assumptions and a process that can be audited for reasonable certainty.

Though this brief overview of valuation methods is doubtless incomplete, it does nevertheless show the diversity of the different approaches which can, when taken together, bring to the process of brand valuation the 'reasonable certainty' that accountants rightly demand.

We at Grand Met believe that shareholders have a right to balance sheets that reflect the cost of purchased brands and where the values are reviewed annually. We also believe that accountants and brand managers will continue to develop new and improved techniques for the valuation of brands, a pressing requirement which the accounting firm Hodgson Impey identified well in an open letter to the UK Accounting Standards Committee (1989):

> Although brand valuation is in its infancy, it should not be discouraged, since generally accepted methods will evolve only through companies considering alternative approaches and applying them in practice.[6]

Adding Shareholder Value

Ultimately however, one must stand back from the accountancy issues and return to what the brand valuation debate is really about: shareholders want to see dividends increase along with their share prices, employees want to work in a successful, growing business, national governments want to see their tax revenues and exports climb, and all these flow from the success of our brands and from their increasing in value.

I am glad to see business schools beginning to address the question of brand values (or 'brand equity', as they more usually put it). For too long we have struggled to measure successful brand management yet, until quite recently, business academics have taken no great part in helping us with this problem. Our dilemma is that while we can measure the immediate profit flow from a brand, it is difficult to establish whether we are truly increasing its capacity for producing long-term profits or merely harvesting the fruits of our predecessors' efforts. In practice market share is still frequently taken as the critical index of success. Each of our brands is seen as being in a sort of competition organised around a league table and because we know that brand leaders are usually more profitable than the followers, the number twos do well enough but below number three brands have to struggle to pay their way at all. Market share performance is seen as the key indicator of brand success. Of course, market share *is* important but smart marketing people are adept at redefining the market to flatter their brand's performance and, overall, an absolute preoccupation with market share can lead to severe self-delusion. Worse still, the pursuit of market share can result in short-term promotional activities that can fatally damage a brand in the long term. Coupons and other consumer price reductions at point-of-sale need to be used with care if they are used at all.

Analysing the brand's contribution to profit can give a rather more useful index of success, but again it is still short-term in nature. However, such analysis helps provide focus and it can produce some of the data necessary for brand valuation. It can also assist the planning process for the immediate period, though difficulties can arise in the longer term. For example: how much should one spend to maximise the profit for this year and how does this relate to the sum needed to maximise the long-term discounted cash flow? Marketing science is not yet close to solving such problems, but it is still worth posing the questions. Indeed, one would not be serving one's shareholders well if one did not.

I believe that brand profit contribution or PLE (product line earnings) as some call it, is the first faltering step towards the proper use of brand valuation and the wider concept of brand equity in the brand management process. Equity is ultimately what the brand manager has to build; when a brand manager takes charge of a brand, that brand has an inherited equity and a stream of earnings; both must be enlarged and management needs to be able to measure progress in real terms. Focusing on short-term market share or on profit shifts is not enough. When people ask me whether I look for long-term or immediate profits I simply say 'Yes' because, clearly, I must look for both. What other answer is there? Grand Met

(a)   (b)

Illustration 5.2

Two more outstanding brands from the Grand Metropolitan portfolio – the company's spirits portfolio is a real treasure chest of international power brands.

is not a short-term business, but we do not forsake the profits we can make today for profits in the future.

I would therefore encourage marketing experts and the accountancy profession to work together to see how brand valuation measurement can be improved. Fortunately, great efforts are now being made to research brand equity in both financial and marketing terms by business schools and others in the USA and UK[7] and I wish them every success. Brand equity enhances not only shareholder value but the prosperity of all involved. We need to know more about it.

Notes

1. Financial Acounting Standards Board, *Elements of Financial Statements of Business Enterprises*, Statement of Financial Accounting Concepts No 3 (Stamdford, Conneticut, 1980).
2. Accounting Principles Board, *Intangible Assets*, Opinion No 17 (New York, 1970).

3. Interbrand, *Brands, An International Review* (London: *Mercury Books*, 1990).

4. Chris Macrae, *World Class Brands* (Wokingham, England: *Addison Wesley*, May 1991).

5. Peter H. Farquhar, Julia Y. Han and Yuji Ijiri, *Recognising and Measuring Brand Assets*, Working Paper, Carnegie Mellon University, May 1991.

6. Hodgson Impey, *An Open Letter to the UK Accounting Standards Committee*, p. 3, 28 February 1989.

7. Christopher Parratt and Keith Holloway, *The Value of Brands*, Brand and Goodwill Accounting Strategies, Chapter 5, ed. Michael Power, 1990.

POWER BRANDING IN THE AUTOMOTIVE INDUSTRY

6

Professor Werner Niefer
Former Chairman
MERCEDES-BENZ AG

One indisputable truth about markets is that they are always changing. The cause of such change, whether it be a major upheaval or a minor adjustment, can normally be identified fairly readily. Changes in the market place can come about as a result of a wide range of factors including the introduction of new legal standards and regulations or shifts in customer needs. Political events play a rôle, as do any changes in the economic situation or in exchange parity. Aggressive competitors, new brands and innovative ideas also have an important influence on the market. Trends in fashion or what might be called 'the spirit of the times' can also play a decisive rôle in changing market structures, attitudes and requirements.

Clearly, the earlier that market changes are recognised and their causes analysed and evaluated, the quicker it is that market opportunities can be identified and potential dangers averted. Once change has been recognised, businesses have plenty of weaponry at their disposal to ensure that they can take advantage of such change. New product launches, price restructuring programmes, alterations in trading activity, investments in targeted sales promotion and advertising

103

Mercedes-Benz

Illustration 6.1

The Mercedes logo is a very well-recognised symbol throughout the world and has come to represent the best in quality, reliability, safety and technology.

campaigns can all be used to exploit the market opportunities provided by change.

Although everyone knows that markets change, it is still amazing to see the extent to which change can affect the performance of individual products, brands, companies and even entire industries. There are three main reasons for this:

(i) Change, by its very nature, means that existing norms of behaviour will no longer apply – consequently, assessing the future effects of change on one's own business with any degree of accuracy can be very difficult to do in practice. It is clearly nonsensical to make long-term business decisions on the assumption that the effects of change are wholly predictable. But, on the other hand, if decisions are delayed until the effects on the market have become clear, counter-measures can be too late to be of any use.

(ii) Even if change is recognised and the probable consequences of such change accurately analysed, the time required to alter products, particularly in a business such as car manufacturing which has very long lead times, may be too long for any response to be effective.

(iii) It is human nature to suppress unpleasant truths which do not fit into our usual pattern of thinking and behaviour and to underestimate dangers which have not yet become apparent. 'Beating about the bush' is as prevalent in business as it is in politics and, regrettably, this tendency to ignore the consequences of change often means that opportunities to benefit therefrom are lost.

Of course, there are ways of overcoming all these problems and for the automobile industries of Europe and to some extent too of America, it is now time to find out what these are.

Clearly, there are no guaranteed paths to success, though instead of just reacting to market changes as they happen, it is surely better to be proactive and adopt a strategy which will actively influence events. Simply to wait until disaster strikes and then to call in the government for protection is the worst possible option.

The Market is neither Private Property nor a Mystery

The world automobile market is currently in a state of considerable flux and this is likely to continue for quite some time yet. The only prevailing certainty is that nothing can be taken for granted in the automobile market, a market which is a highly complex and one which is not governed solely (as is the case in many other markets) by a simple relationship between the wishes of consumers and the quality of the products supplied.

There are many important factors influencing the automobile market which are outside the normal market dynamics of supply and demand. Among these are, for example, state assistance for exports on the one hand and state imposition of import restrictions on the other. Customs duties, taxes and levies on passenger cars and commercial vehicles are, by their very number and variety, proof of an administrative determination to influence the market which cannot be underestimated. Governments further influence the automobile market and car usage by putting taxes on vehicles and fuel. The general economic situation also plays an important rôle in the automobile market and the motor industry's prospects depend to a large extent on the economy and on whether consumers judge economic prospects optimistically or pessimistically. In addition, private disposable income affects both the consumer's disposition to buy and the manufacturer's ability to be flexible on price.

Another important influence on both the automobile industry and its customers is the rules and regulations governing exhaust and particulate emissions and fuel consumption: in the USA, for example, this is used as a limiting factor for fleet sizes. Construction and registration regulations may also vary markedly from country to country, all of which adds to the bulk of legislation literature and makes the job of the manufacturer more complex and, at times, more uncertain.

The tradition or underlying culture and attitudes of a manufacturer are frequently underestimated as factors which influence the ability to respond to change; in my experience they can have a decisive influence and can, for example, make a business inflexible and obscure its view of changing market conditions. For example, the car industry in the USA has never placed much value on export and largely confines its activities to the domestic market. As a result, even though the large American companies now have a network of overseas subsidiaries, these do not compensate them for the important slice of the domestic market which is now represented by imports – in 1990 a good 40 per cent.

On the other hand, tradition can be an important part of the personality of a brand. If customers identify with these traditional characteristics then they can provide the brand with appeal and continuity. Mercedes-Benz is an example of the productive use of tradition.

The New Dimensions of the Market

The well-documented 'Japanese challenge' is not the only one to which motor manufacturers in the USA and Europe have to respond. Indeed, there is a risk of our not paying enough attention to other important issues while we continue to stare, dazzled, at the diligent car makers from the land of the rising sun.

Many companies believe that the problem of Japanese competition is cost-related and conclude that the only way to compete is to reduce costs of production (and therefore car prices) without diminishing either quality or technical standards. However, the primary issue facing motor producers is still the one which has always been with us: how to build cars which make owners happy and satisfied. And it is here that branding has a powerful rôle to play.

Today, in the automotive market, the different brands in each segment of the market broadly match each other in terms of technological standards, overall quality and even design. This makes it increasingly difficult for manufacturers to define the outstanding features of their brands and clearly distinguish and differentiate them from their competitors. In response, manufacturers need to introduce technical innovations, quality improvements, new styling features and other advantages within each price band in order to secure the success of their brands.

Customers in the 1990s are more sophisticated than ever before. Since the basic need for mobility is easily satisfied they now demand uniqueness, exclusivity and special features. This change in values is part of a new individualism. Most motorists want pleasure, adventure and the fascination of choice when they buy a car; mere mobility is a basic requirement but is far from being enough to satisfy today's consumers.

Manufacturers have answered this requirement by offering family and sports cars, estate cars, vans, coupés and convertibles with many variations and different engine outputs. As a consequence, they have redefined the motor vehicle as a means of achieving and expressing an individual lifestyle; if we disregard this desire for individuality voiced by customers, we are bound to lose market share and market appeal.

Another challenge facing both the motor manufacturer and the motorist is that of environmental protection – the conservation of the planet itself for future generations is no longer a minority issue and, even before the year 2000, it might easily become the most significant issue facing every citizen. The cost of keeping the air, water and soil clean, of processing and disposing of waste, of protecting the climate, of recycling valuable raw materials and of securing global energy requirements will account for an ever-growing share of individual incomes. Motor vehicles play an increasingly large rôle in public awareness of environmental issues. In big cities and metropolitan areas as well as on the major traffic arteries, traffic congestion is a prominent issue on the 'green' agenda.

The automotive industry cannot afford to ignore the conflict between the desire for individual freedom and the need to be environmentally friendly. If we are to achieve as little restriction of mobility as possible while protecting the environment, this inevitably means that some form of reconciliation must be reached between economic and ecological objectives. Some sceptics may argue that such a reconciliation is impossible, but they are wrong. We have to find a way to make such a reconciliation happen because otherwise the likelihood is that uncompromising government intervention will follow, a development which would imply a drastic shift in the democratic structure of our society.

So, overall, the measures open to motor manufacturers to cope with all these new market realities are as follows:

(i) We must reduce costs so as to be able to offer quality and innovation at competitive prices.

(ii) We must maintain an edge in technology and cost-efficiency in order to give the customer a distinctive product.

(iii) We must help to solve environmental and traffic problems with robust and effective contributions, whilst preserving mobility for the individual.

These are the new dimensions of the market in which the motor industry operates. All motor manufacturers have scope to respond to these requirements.

The Position of Mercedes-Benz

In 1990 we produced 574 000 vehicles. This is only 1.6 per cent of the total world car production, but it makes Mercedes-Benz the world's largest manufacturer of high-quality cars. Our commercial vehicle production in 1990 was 259 000 transporters, trucks, buses, Unimogs and MB tractors. This is no more than 2 per cent of total world production of commercial vehicles, yet it makes Mercedes-Benz the largest truck manufacturer in the world.

Illustration 6.2
The Mercedes-Benz SK series won Truck of the Year in 1990. This series of trucks has been specially designed to meet the transport and distribution requirements of the single European market.

There is however more to selling vehicles than quantity, and Mercedes-Benz also occupies the number one spot in the image rating of brands, a factor of which both we and our customers are proud. The Mercedes-Benz name has been associated with quality for 105 years but success and prestige cannot be inherited – one has to work hard for them. These are our credentials for the last forty years:

Figure 6.1   Mercedes-Benz key indicators

	1950	1970	1990
Turnover in DM billions	0.5	10.5	59.8
Car production	34 000	280 000	574 000
Commercial vehicle production	8000	196 000	259 000
Employees	27 000	159 000	231 000
Investments in DM billions	0.005	0.976	3.500

Mercedes-Benz AG, now a corporate unit of the Daimler-Benz high technology concern, is the oldest car manufacturer in the world. This heritage brings an obligation to carry on our traditions of excellence into the future. Being number one is not as easy as numbers two, three or four might think! number one is never allowed to make any mistakes, has a responsibility to be successful and is mercilessly denounced for any slip-up. Doing well cannot be a one-off achievement but, rather, the minimum required to fulfil expectations. Any manufacturer claiming to be number 1 is clearly expected to be especially competent; but reputation and image are like capital in a bank account from which both competitive action and one's personal mistakes are constantly making withdrawals. If we do not make regular deposits in the form of superior performance then one day we will go into the red.

For all these reasons, competence lies at the very heart of the Mercedes-Benz brand philosophy. Yet competence alone is not enough to win and keep the interest and loyalty of customers; Mercedes-Benz also makes an effort to win affection. This is not always easy since successful businesses are more likely to seem cold and arrogant. We try to avoid such traits and consider them to be a sign of weakness and lack of self-confidence. Within our company our regard and concern for our customers and our wish to satisfy their requirements are genuine and deeply felt.

What then are the fundamental values of the Mercedes-Benz brand, the qualities that first occur to people when they are asked their opinion of Mercedes-Benz? We believe them to be quality, reliability, safety, forward-thinking technology and, in the field of commercial vehicles, overall economy. An additional concern is the environmental compatibility of both the production process and of our products, something that has been at the forefront of the company's thinking for many years.

Mercedes-Benz has no wish to be overtaken by anyone in the maintenance of these fundamental values. Moreover, these values have the same significance in every one of the 170 countries where Mercedes-Benz vehicles are sold and driven. If the best of our competitors comes close to equalling our standards, then we make extraordinary efforts to improve

Illustration 6.3
The new Mercedes SL combines classic elegance with excitement and power. Design and technology have been brought together perfectly to create a car of exceptional quality and performance.

them yet again. The new S-class vehicles are the most recent proof of this commitment.

But we also try to give our fundamental values an extra sparkle by adding to them those extra contemporary qualities and values which customers demand from a Mercedes. These include sportiness, up-to-date interior and exterior design, comfort, handling characteristics and, just as importantly, exclusivity. Mercedes-Benz has also established a service and care system for its products which aims to increase the customers' benefit from and enjoyment of their vehicles while relieving them of the burden of maintenance.

The Brand is the Answer

Customers form a picture of the brand from their experience of the products and services sold under a brand. Every message they receive from the manufacturer helps to fill in the details of this picture. If the brand gives customers good answers to their questions, desires and needs, then all is well. Thus manufacturers must do everything they can to make a brand attractive and convincing and to avoid anything which does not suit the desired image of the brand.

Manufacturers must therefore have a clear idea of what customers expect. They must also constantly try to ensure that the product meets the customers' needs. If this is neglected in any way, it leads to a depreciation in the value of the brand and confuses customers. Frequent inconsistencies or contradictions between the customers' demands and the reality of the product eventually lead to a loss of trust and an unwillingness to buy the product.

But it is not only important to recognise and respond to the customers' needs. Every measure taken by the company must also make a clear contribution to the desired image of the

Illustration 6.4
The new S class provides an image of calm elegance and sophistication. The distinctive Mercedes badge stands proudly on the vehicle bonnet identifying the car with everything that the Mercedes brand has come to represent.

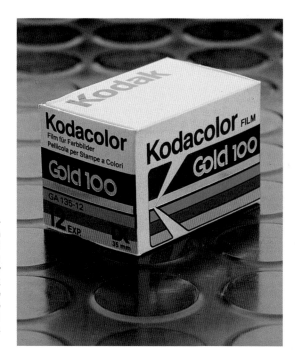

Plate 1
Kodak is one of the few companies bold enough to take an entirely abstract name and invest it with brand equity. The powerful intellectual property rights residing in the Kodak brand name and identity have been carefully nurtured since the brand's launch in 1888 and have contributed greatly to its brand power.

Plate 2
Bass have been brewers since 1777 so when in 1876 they obtained the first registered trade mark in Britain for their red triangle device, they were already centenarians. The Bass brand remains of key importance to the group and is recognised around the world as the number one British ale.

Plate 3

The Quaker Oats Company is a broadly based food company but its core product is its original product, Quaker Oatmeal. The Quaker brand identity has evolved over time to stay relevant and appealing to generation after generation of consumers. Quaker calls its brands its 'Value Portfolio' and sees brand power as the means to achieve lasting corporate success.

Plate 4

Hertz is a true power brand in the car rental market and is proof of the fact that branding can work equally well with services as it does with 'things'.

Plate 5
Kellogg's has an intensely `brand-centric' corporate culture and this is reflected in the quality and strength of the Kellogg's brand, which has made the breakfast cereals market its own.

Plate 6
The recent reduction in the price of Marlboro in the US was brought about to restore the price differential between Marlboro and cheap discount brands to a more realistic level — Marlboro's phenomenal brand power has not been affected to any extent.

Plate 7
Lea & Perrins Worcestershire Sauce has a strong worldwide follow-ing and has the characteristics of market leadership, stability and brand strength that will enable it to maintain its brand power status for years to come.

Plate 8
The Guinness brand identity is communicated consistently and clearly across the full range of Guinness stout products.

Plate 9
Powerful international brands like Cinzano which have a strong consumer franchise can command premium prices and, if managed appropriately, can become very valuable.

Plate 10
Malibu is a strong brand within the international drinks portfolio of Grand Metropolitan plc, and is featured in the company's annual report and accounts.

When David told me he'd give me the sun, the moon and the stars, I told him he and my Baileys were just fine for the moment.

BAILEYS
RAISES THE ART OF THE EVERYDAY.™

Plate 11
Baileys has been one of the great marketing success stories of the last few years and Grand Metropolitan's shareholders have every right to be proud of what it has achieved.

Plate 12
One of the brands acquired as part of Grand Met's takeover of Pillsbury was Green Giant. It is difficult for even the finest brands to add value to basic commodity products, like canned vegetables, but Green Giant has proved that it can be done.

Plate 13
One of the world's most prestigious brands of scotch, J & B Rare, has a powerful heritage, having been originally founded in 1749.

Plate 14
Galbani produces a wide range of cheese products for Italian consumers and is the biggest manufacturer of cheese in Italy. The brand name of Galbani represents the best in Italian cheese.

Plate 15

Certain cheeses, such as the mozzarella shown here, appear in well-known shapes and sizes to promote recognition and recall.

Plate 16

Some Italian cheeses are known by a specific product brand name rather than a generic name. Galbani's crescenza cheese, for example, has been branded as Certosa. This means that any advertising spend put behind Certosa helps to build awareness of this particular brand rather than the crescenza segment as a whole.

Plate 17
With provolone cheese the Galbani name is used to provide an endorsement of tradition, reliability and quality.

Plate 18
One of Galbani's best-known branded cheeses, not just in Italy but around the world, is Bel Paese. Its unusual name, distinctive round shape and intricate label design are brand equities which millions of consumers recognise.

Plate 19

When Galbani launched gorgonzola into the UK market it was decided that the product should be launched under a brand name rather than the generic name. Dolcelatte has been a great success and proves that a commodity product like gorgonzola can be branded successfully.

Plate 20

The packaging of Galbani's taleggio is highly distinctive, with the Galbani logo shown prominently so that consumers can see which of the cheeses on display are from the Galbani family.

Plate 21
Every day thousands of Galbani vans, or camioncini, visit 230 000 outlets across the country delivering fresh cheese and salami products. The striking yellow and green vans together with the famous red and white Galbani logo are a regular sight in Italy's towns and villages and have become a part of Italian daily life.

UNITED COLORS
OF BENETTON.

Plate 22
The Benetton logo is used consistently and extensively across all of Benetton's products and promotional items.

Plate 23
Benetton shops have always been designed with the consumer in mind. The interiors are light, airy and informal, making shopping for clothes a pleasurable experience. This shop in Milan in Piazza San Babila was opened in May 1993.

Plate 24
Benetton's advertising has always been designed to provoke comment on important issues of the day. This poster advertisment of a black boy and white girl hugging each other showed how children, regardless of race, can be united in friendship and love.

Plates 25 and 26
Benetton advertising has often raised awareness on issues that others might wish to disguise. These two posters make a powerful statement about the horror of oil pollution and the point-lessness of war.

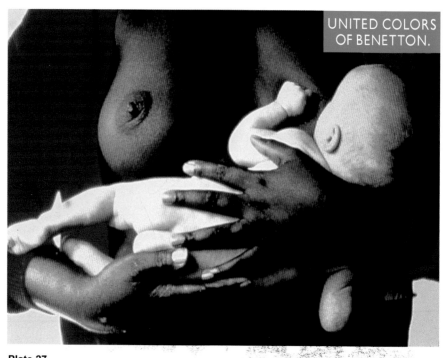

Plate 27
This poster of a black mother suckling a white baby caused considerable controversy when it was launched but served to emphasise the fact we are all human beings, whatever our colour or creed.

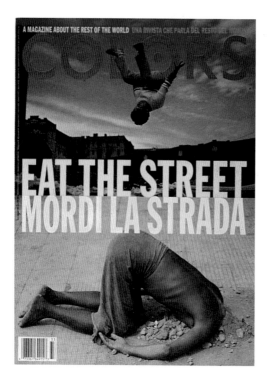

Plate 28
Colors was first published in 1991 as a new magazine designed to discuss important themes relating to culture and the environment.

Plate 29
Benetton has also invested heavily in Formula One. The Benetton team has had considerable success in the Grand Prix circuits of the world. Formula One provides a perfect medium through which to communicate the excitement and power of the Benetton brand to people all around the world.

Plate 30
Benetton has been an important sponsor of many sports, including rugby in Italy. The Benetton team won the Italian Championship in 1992 and were runners-up in 1993.

Plate 31
M&M's is one of the most powerful world brands owned by Mars.

Plate 32
Whiskas was launched in 1959 and now holds the position as the best selling pet food brand in the world. The Whiskas brand identity is used powerfully in communications materials, as is demonstrated by this advertisement for the German market.

Plate 33
The success of the Pedigree dog foods brand is founded upon the endorsement it receives from top dog breeders around the world.

Plate 34
The Mars Bar, with its unique combination of milk, glucose, malt from barley and thick chocolate, has been a leading force in the confectionery markets of the world since its launch in 1932. Most recently it has expanded its sphere of influence to include the former Soviet Union — shown here is an advertisement in the Russian market produced in 1992.

Plate 35

Mars has a policy of developing and protecting international brand names. Snickers is a good example of a strong international brand.

THE BREAK, THE SNACK, TWIX® FITS.

Plate 36

Another powerful brand in the Mars portfolio.

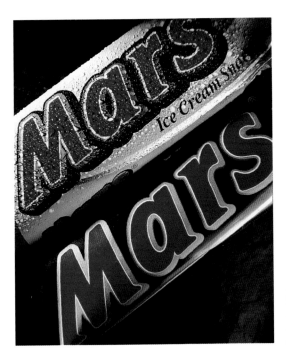

Plate 37
The launch of Mars Bar Ice Cream
has proved to be one of the most
successful line extensions in the
confectionery market.

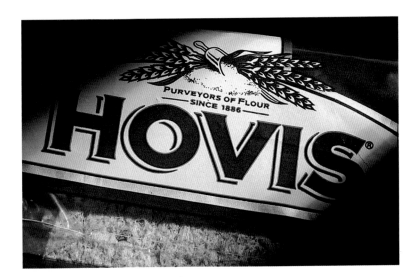

Plate 38
Hovis is a strong brand of bread in the UK market. The owner of the brand, Ranks
Hovis McDougall, valued its entire portfolio of brands in 1988 and capitalised this
value on the balance sheet. This was the first time that both acquired and `home-
grown' brands were included in a balance sheet brand valuation.

Plate 39
Ritz crackers was one of the major brands acquired by BSN from RJR Nabisco in 1988. BSN has a policy of including all its major acquired brands on the group balance sheet.

Plate 40
Steinlager is perhaps New Zealand's most famous brand. It is sold in over 60 countries around the world and is promoted heavily in sports sponsorship. Lion Nathan, the largest brewer in Australia and New Zealand, has a policy of including its brands on the balance sheet and is proud of its record of building brand value.

Plate 41
Pacific Dunlop is one of Australia's largest industrial companies with interests in many countries around the world. It also has a valuable brand portfolio. Adidas and Slazenger are two famous sports brands that Pacific Dunlop owns in the Pacific market place.

Plate 42
The Whyte & Mackay portfolio of scotch whisky was sold by Lonrho to Brent Walker and was then acquired by American Brands. The portfolio is now managed by Gallaher in the UK on behalf of itsUS parent, American Brands.

Plate 43

The value of the Gucci brand was fought over in the courts when the Gucci family claimed successfully that Paolo Gucci was infringing the trade mark rights and hence undermining the value of the Gucci brand. The importance of brand valuation was accepted by the UK High Court as being of fundamental importance to the outcome of the case.

Plate 44

The Kraft company was acquired by Philip Morris for $12.9 billion in 1988. Although best known for its processed cheese, the brand is now used to support a broad range of products, albeit with strong dairy associations.

Plate 45
Coca-Cola is the world's number one brand. Now over one hundred years old it has been meticulously managed throughout its life but in a manner which has ensured that its original brand values have been maintained consistently and clearly. Coca-Cola is the quintessential power brand.

Plate 46
The McDonald's franchising concept has been a tremendous success not only in the US but throughout the world. The success of McDonald's has now been copied by a number of fast food operators but McDonald's is still considered to be the world leader.

Plate 47
Heineken is a true power brand in the international beer market. It dominates its home market in Holland but is also a powerful force in the USA, UK, Indonesia and the Caribbean.

Plate 48
Swatch has been one of the major branding success stories of the last decade. Launched in 1983 as a cheap, cleverly marketed alternative to mainstream watches, Swatch has restored the Swiss industry's confidence in producing high-volume time-pieces.

brand. If the co-ordination and strict brand direction necessary to achieve this are neglected, there will be difficult times ahead for the company. The success of its efforts will be limited and the cost will be high. Since the brand is the most valuable asset owned by the company and the fate of the company lies with the brand, full commitment to the brand is absolutely essential.

From the Mercedes-Benz brand customers expect to have their individual needs fulfilled in a way compatible with social responsibility. They expect to pay a price commensurate with the highest standards of quality and technology. Moreover, customers place greater demands on the image leader than on other brands, and if their demands are not met by the image leader then the disappointment is greater than it would be in the case of a lesser brand.

That is why at Mercedes-Benz two brand objectives have an equally high priority. The first objective is flexibility in responding to the personal wishes and needs of our customers worldwide. The second is that we play an exemplary rôle in providing fundamental values such as quality, reliability, safety and in accepting joint responsibility for solving all problems related to the motor vehicle.

No one driving a Mercedes wishes to disregard the environment, safety or traffic, yet, at the same time, they do not want problems related to the environment, safety or traffic to force them to sacrifice individual mobility or driving pleasure. They expect a leading brand to offer a comprehensive choice, the best the industry can currently produce and the promise of direction for the future. This brand objective has been met by Mercedes-Benz.

Mercedes-Benz recognises five factors which influence the success of a brand: product, production, service, motivation and communication.

The product factor

The product factor concerns the research, development and design of the individual products and of the whole product range. At present the brand offers 56 different car models as

Illustration 6.5
Mercedes cars have always had a particular style and elegance that sets them apart
from other cars on the road.

well as various Sportline versions. They range from the super
economy diesel car 190 D to the super sports car 600 SL with a
V12 engine. With the launch of the new S-class in Spring 1991,
Mercedes-Benz set the new technical standards for the 1990s.
A further step then came with the launch of the 300er
Convertible.

The Commercial Vehicles Division, with its full-line vehicle
range, is also a major contributor to the success of the
Mercedes-Benz brand. Its product range from the transporter
to the heavy truck, from the bus for long-distance travel and
public transport through to the Unimog, the vehicle for
municipal and fire services, to industrial engines. Space does
not however allow for a full appreciation of the Commercial
Vehicle Division, which is as important for the company as it
is for the market; instead, I have focused in this appraisal of
the Mercedes-Benz brand mainly on personal cars.

Within the personal car range massive efforts have been
made in the area of environmental compatibility. In 1986

Illustration 6.6
Mercedes buses represent the latest in design and technological innovation. The O 404 range shown here was introduced in late 1991.

Mercedes-Benz became the first car manufacturer to fit its vehicles for the German market with a catalytic converter as a standard feature. Now, durable high-performance closed-loop catalytic converters purify the exhaust emissions to a greater extent than is required by law.

Since 1982 our exceptionally economical diesel cars have been available with noise-encapsulated engines, and since 1989 they have been on offer with sharply reduced emissions of pollutants and particles. Since Autumn 1990 they have been available with oxidation catalytic converters and exhaust gas recirculation on request. This means that Mercedes-Benz diesel cars are not only on average 20 per cent more economical in terms of fuel consumption than petrol driven cars fitted with catalytic converters, but they are also at least as environmentally compatible.

Mercedes-Benz is also gradually integrating ecology into economy. The aim is to produce energy-saving cars which also save on raw materials and which can be almost totally recycled at the end of their life span. The fuel consumption of all Mercedes-Benz cars has already been reduced by a total of 25 per cent in the last 10 years.

The brand also has the leading position in both active and passive safety. Three safety features which were first introduced by Mercedes-Benz have been very successful in the market: over 7 million automatic seat belt tensioners, over 2.5 million ABS (brakes) and approximately 750 000 airbag systems have already been fitted in Mercedes-Benz vehicles.

Future product innovations will also be strictly directed towards safety, reducing demands on the driver, compatibility with the environment and measures to save energy and raw materials.

The production factor

The second factor, the production factor, aims to achieve through innovative techniques, a more flexible production system and a reduction in manufacturing costs. As long as strict quality standards are adhered to, there are no restrictions on innovation in this area. New methods of production, working processes and logistics systems are being introduced into our German plants and, in addition, new ventures in the production and sales co-operation areas are being pursued overseas along with increased sourcing of materials from abroad. Overall, we are clear that the price competitiveness of the brand can only be maintained through a reduction in costs.

The service factor

The sales and technical customer services areas, comprising 5800 outlets worldwide for cars and commercial vehicles, are part of the service factor. Extended customer care services are becoming increasingly important and we have responded through features such as customer credit cards (the 'Mercedes card'), warranty programmes (the 'Touring Guarantee' and used-car warranties) and our rapidly expanding leasing and financing services.

The motivation factor

It is apparent that the culture practised within the company is that which is ultimately experienced by the customer. In producing such a culture the importance of the motivation factor cannot be overstressed. Here, it is up to the personnel department to establish a system of apprenticeships and training for employees, to uphold the principle of 'the right person for the job', to establish clear aims and management principles which are based upon exemplary rôle models and not on the exercise of power. The smooth running and organisation of work is as important to employees as the opportunity to develop the full range of their abilities. Every company which has examined the evidence will confirm that genuine motivation results in a reduction in costs.

The communication factor

The fifth factor for success is communication and the more successfully and precisely our communications efforts interpret the character of the brand the more successful our brand is. Communication is not however a one-way street; for Mercedes-Benz communication means both understanding and making oneself understood. It means talking to customers, the press and the general public and presenting a well-defined image, but it also means creating relationships. Of course building such relationships can be initiated through courageous advertising which conveys competence and excites enthusiasm. Accurate and informative press information has a part to play. But there is also communication through inviting customers to the plants, to the sales offices and to cultural and sporting events such as the automotive competitions in which Mercedes-Benz is taking part with its touring cars and sports prototypes – the new 'Silver Arrows'.

Illustration 6.7
Mercedes is heavily involved in the world of motor racing and has a highly successful record. Shown here is the Mercedes-Benz C11 which achieved great success in the Sportscar World Championship.

Progress in the Right Direction

It is satisfying to be able to take part in shaping the future. At Mercedes-Benz we are well aware that the future cannot just repeat the past. In the future our lifestyles may differ radically from those of today, just as today's world is quite different from that of our parents and our grandparents. It may even be, in the future, that the whole concept of mobility is changed. So we will have new aims and will need to follow new paths, a process which creates many challenges for a dynamic brand such as ours: producing vehicles which are acceptable both to our customers and the environment, helping to improve traffic safety, solving the traffic problems in large cities and conurbations, achieving a new co-ordination between the various traffic systems, overcoming the vicious circle of cost-price. There are the challenges involved in the development of free trade throughout the world and the evening out of the differences between North and South. Finally, the responsibility for hundreds of thousands of jobs and of our shareholders cannot be separated from these tasks.

The research department of Daimler-Benz AG, and the corporate units of the group including Mercedes-Benz, are working hard on projects in all the areas I have described, for example:

(i)   In the field of the improvement of traffic economy we are working on solutions for Stuttgart, Berlin, Hong Kong and Singapore.

(ii)   We have fully developed 250 vehicles to test alternative drive systems, including engines powered by electricity and water.

(iii)   Expenditure on environmental protection amounted to DM 180 million in 1990 and our expenditure for environmentally compatible product fittings and production equipment amounted to another DM 700 million.

Mercedes-Benz is dedicated to helping individuals keep their freedom of mobility. To this end we are using all our creativity, knowledge and ability to turn technical progress into progress for humanity as a whole.

THE EMERGENCE OF RETAIL BRAND POWER 7

Terry Leahy
Marketing Director
TESCO GROUP PLC

Introduction

The emergence of retail brand power may be a comparatively recent phenomenon but the emergence of retailing power is not. Retailing powerhouses like Sears, Woolworths and the British Co-operative movement have been in existence for generations and, in their heyday, had an almost institutional status within society. Indeed, branded products of one sort or another have been bought and sold by retailers for decades yet most textbooks on marketing and on branding have, at least until very recently, tended to ignore the retailer's influence on branding. This omission is surprising since it is clear that retailing has had a profound impact on branding techniques for far more than just the last few years.

Given the importance of retailing to the branding process, why has it taken industry observers and academics so long to realise that retailers have such an important rôle to play? My own view is that these observers and academics have taken retailers and the retailing function for granted. Retailers have been seen as middlemen, a distribution channel, an inconvenient necessity to get products to the consumer. Branding has been seen as the exclusive domain of the manufacturer and nothing to do with the retailer. These attitudes are, however, changing fast largely due to the rapid rise to

121

prominence of the multiple food retailers. The growth of own label branding in markets like the UK, France and Germany has challenged traditional thinking in those countries.

The purpose of this chapter is to set out how retail brand power has come about and to use the experiences of one leading British food retailer, Tesco, to see how retail branding actually works in practice.

Consumer Perceptions about Shopping

At first sight it would seem that very few consumers could actually enjoy going through the weekly chore of shopping for food. Shopping for a large family can be physically draining, dull, repetitive, stressful, time-consuming and expensive. Yet consumers do have to go through with it because, after all, everyone has to eat. The challenge for retailers is to make the experience more pleasurable. The results of the strenuous efforts made by British food retailers to improve their retail 'offer' can be seen today in research which shows that a majority of people now actually enjoy shopping!

How has this come about? What is it that retailers have done to change radically consumer perceptions about shopping? The answers to questions such as these may be found by examining two developments which have had a profound effect on the retailing industry: first, format evolution and secondly, brand evolution.

Format evolution

It was recognised that one of the fundamental irritants for consumers had long been the unhelpful format of most retail outlets. Retailers therefore took steps to address the inadequacies of high street food shopping and provide consumers with a better environment. It may seem with hindsight that each step in the evolution of the retail format was an obvious one to take but the fact is that each such step was at the time considered to be a bold move.

Illustration 7.1

One of the great milestones of the 'retail revolution' was the introduction of self-service shopping. Jack Cohen, the founder of Tesco, managed to achieve rapid growth for Tesco by converting many of his stores to a self-service format. Shown here is a Tesco self-service retail outlet in the 1940s.

It is ironic that the first milestone, the introduction of self-service, was only made possible by manufacturers' success in pre-packing products of consistently good quality. Removing the need to have shop assistants serving customers saved time for the shopper and money for the retailer. People even today talk fondly of the old-style service yet it was and is an inefficient and expensive means of serving the customer and is not seen in the modern food store save as a special sideshow.

The second milestone was made possible by the savings from the first: savings made from introducing self-service shopping enabled retailers to reduce prices. The effect of reducing prices was to increase volumes and this, in turn, enabled retailers not only to cover their overheads on thinner margins but also provided them with the opportunity to buy larger quantities from their suppliers at better unit prices. The savings made from bulk buying were invested to produce more volume which produced more savings, and so on. So began the familiar spiral which eventually brought about the development of price discounting which was the hallmark of the early food multiples. Most of this activity was taking place at a time in the 1950s when food spend was almost 40 per cent of discretionary expenditure, so the prospect of cheaper prices clearly addressed a very major problem for the food shopper: the disproportionately large share which food shopping then took of the weekly budget.

The third milestone coincided with the advent of widespread car ownership. The ability of consumers to travel great distances meant that stores could be built on 'out-of-town' sites away from the expense and congestion of the High Street. Customers could access these new stores with relative comfort, thereby removing a lot of the time and drudgery

Illustration 7.2

The self service format enabled retailers to save overheads. These savings were passed on to consumers in the form of lower prices. Tesco was at the forefront of developments in this field. Throughout the 1960s Tesco increased its turnover tenfold, largely as a result of its successful price-oriented brand proposition. Pictured here is a shop window from the 1960s where the emphasis on price is clearly visible.

from the shopping experience. Retailers even threw in cheap petrol as a draw. Even though the advantages of these large out-of-town sites are evident today it is interesting to note that when they were first developed it was often not the established High Street multiples who made the first move. The established retailers were not only anxious to protect their existing business but also felt that investing in out-of-town sites was inherently risky whereas investing in the High Street was not.

Out-of-town stores were, of course, self-service and the goods sold in them were priced very competitively, which meant that the fourth milestone in format evolution could take place. Out-of-town stores could be built large enough to offer a very wide range of goods thereby offering consumers the prospect of a 'one-stop shop'. Most customers were only too happy to give up the dubious pleasure of having to visit half a dozen shops along the High Street on every occasion that the larder had to be re-stocked.

Each of these separate changes has had its pioneers; self-service started in America, discounting in Britain and Germany, one-stop shopping in France. None of these developments ever really became the property of one particular retail brand but formed instead, by the 1970s, a communal platform upon which individual retail brands could be built.

Brand evolution

Brand evolution, that is the development of distinctive retailer brands, became a strategy of those retailers who recognised, either through the benefit of consumer research or as a result of divine inspiration, that consumers select which stores they go to for a wide variety of reasons but primarily because of the following:

(i) the quality of the products
(ii) the convenience of the location
(iii) the efficiency of the shopping trip
(iv) the quality of the store itself

By satisfying these consumer needs in a distinctive and appropriate manner, a *retailer* could build a powerful and differentiated retail brand. Retailers who branded their 'offer' effectively were better able to attract and command consumer loyalty. Let us examine each of the consumer needs in turn.

Product quality

Most retailers stock the leading manufacturer brands in any particular product category. Since such brands are all seen at all major stores they say nothing about retailer quality. Instead, the shopper assesses retailer quality by examining unbranded fresh food and the retailer's 'own brand' products. It is hardly surprising, therefore, that retailers have learned to give these product categories such a high profile. It is, after all, one of the most immediate ways in which one store can differentiate itself from another. And there are no short cuts to own brand quality. It requires investment in research, in technology, in product development and in product marketing and on a scale similar to that

Illustration 7.3

Shoppers assess the quality of a retail brand by looking at the quality of unbranded fresh food and own brand products. Retailers consequently have spent considerable time and effort developing own brand products of the highest quality. Tesco's range of Healthy Eating products is a good example of this trend.

employed by the manufacturer. We shall return to this theme a little later.

The convenience of the location

Moving out of town makes sense but where to exactly? Finding a site in the right location can produce double the turnover of a similarly sized but badly placed site. Finding the right site requires particular skills in research, in property and in financing. Not all retailers possess these skills to a sufficient extent.

The efficiency of the shopping trip

In a successful modern food superstore around 25 000 customers will come in to the store every week at a time of their choosing to buy the goods they want from a selection of some 20 000 on offer. Customers expect to find whatever they want and, what is more, to find it in peak condition. They expect to locate what they want easily and with no fuss. They expect to be able to move efficiently around the store, to be able to pay promptly and to get away quickly. Designing and building a store capable of doing this job, developing advanced replenishment systems to balance supply and demand effectively and training and managing staff to achieve the highest levels of operational efficiency and customer service can only be obtained as a result of many years of experience and considerable investment.

The quality of the store itself

People go shopping to buy products and the store itself provides the environment within which shopping takes place. The store is, in a sense, like the packaging that surrounds a product and – like any packaging – it has to protect, promote, inform and communicate in order to create an appropriate image. Those retailers bold enough to invest

Illustration 7.4

The 'shopping environment' is very important to consumers. If shoppers enjoy the experience of shopping at a particular store they are likely to return regularly. Tesco has invested millions of pounds ensuring that the Tesco 'shopping environment' is the best available in the market.

in the quality of the buildings and in the overall environment, both inside and outside their stores, have seen the strength and attractiveness of their brand improve significantly.

This process of brand evolution had its origins in the mid-1970s and, after a brief hiccough during the 1979–1981 recession, gathered momentum throughout the 1980s. The phenomenon is an international one but is probably most visible in British retailing as evidenced by the achievements of retailers such as Tesco, Marks & Spencer, Sainsbury and Safeway. The financial restructuring of many of the large US food retailers during the 1980s also resulted in a stronger emphasis being placed on branding, particularly by strong regional chains like Albertsons, Vons, Wegmans and Giant. In Europe, Migros of Switzerland has become a very powerful brand and Auchan, Continent and Carrefour are developing clear brand identities in France and Spain.

The Development of Own Brands

One factor that makes British retailing relatively unusual is the high proportion of own brand sales. Marks & Spencer, for example, stock nothing except own brand. The proportion of own brand food sales of Tesco, Sainsbury and Safeway is around 50 per cent, 55 per cent and 40 per cent respectively. If one were to include unbranded fresh food which is managed entirely by the retailer and directly affects brand image, then the proportion of own brand would be much higher, probably as much as 70 per cent in the case of Tesco.

While own brand is still increasing as a proportion of overall sales, its rate of growth is probably diminishing. The original purpose behind the development of own brand products was to provide a cheaper, value-for-money alternative to the branded market leaders. Since retailers incur little marketing overhead in connection with own brand products they were also a source of extra profit. Occasionally own brand would be used to ensure security of supply in cases where no alternatives were readily available.

With the realisation that the quality of own brand is of special importance in shoppers' choice of store, attention has shifted to the branding potential of own brand. The quality benchmark for an own brand product in the UK is now often set at a level in excess of that of the market leader. (In the food sector, the market leader is often another own brand product, powerful proof of the brand power of retailers.) Retailers like to offer a quality alternative in each major product category and own brand products are used extensively in situations where quality has to be specified and controlled throughout the distribution chain such as in the area of high risk perishable foods. A great deal of product development work is dedicated to the development of exclusive and highly innovative own brand products which can only be purchased from one retailer. For the retailer, developing innovative own brand products is reasonably efficient since the costs involved are relatively low, as too are the risks. New product development for the manufacturer, on the other hand, is fraught with risk and is very costly. Overall, the desire of the

Illustration 7.5

In fresh food quality is essential. Very few manufacturer brands can guarantee the levels of quality and freshness required. Consequently the onus has been on the retailers to lead the way in this field. Shown here is the delicatessen counter at one of Tesco's modern superstores.

retailers to demonstrate their 'quality of product' to consumers by developing a stream of innovative own brand products has been of great benefit to consumers as product choice and quality have improved markedly.

There are still many markets, like fresh fish, fresh poultry and fresh meat, where quality remains a critical concern for customers yet there are very few manufacturer brands in existence in such areas which can provide consumers with appropriate guarantees of quality.

Managing the development and distribution of own brand production on this scale is no small undertaking. Between them, the four leading British food retailers probably employ over 1000 product development and quality control specialists and the same number of buyers and marketing executives. These people fulfil the product management rôle that used to be the exclusive preserve of the manufacturer.

Further personnel and a significant amount of investment is dedicated to the own brand manufacturing facilities. Originally own brand was only produced when capacity allowed it but, increasingly, entire factories and entire companies are dedicated to the production of own brand. The importance and sheer size of own brand production in the UK has led to a situation where some manufacturers dedicate entire facilities to a single retail customer. The return on investment from supplying high quality own brand products is good and is increasing and there is no shortage of manufacturing investment.

Retail Dominance

Effective retail branding should not be confused, as some commentators would have it, with retail dominance. The market share of food and drink enjoyed by Tesco in the UK is around 10 per cent. A share of this size enables Tesco to pursue a vigorous brand-oriented marketing strategy but such a strategy will only succeed if Tesco remains competitive; a 10 per cent market share does not represent retail dominance.

There has also been a suggestion that a 'balance of power' exists between manufacturer and retailer and that one effect of the emergence of retail branding is that the balance has shifted from the former to the latter. This is not so. It seems to me that there is no obvious reason why a balance of power should need to exist (I shall return to this below) and, in any case, manufacturers of branded goods are hardly powerless.

In each major product category the top five UK manufacturers have a far greater market share than the top five UK retailers. Indeed, in most cases the biggest manufacturer controls more of the market than the biggest retailer. This is even more apparent when the full European market is considered. With the development of the European Single Market there has been considerable merger and acquisition activity amongst the major manufacturers. Overall, if in each major product category the top five European manufacturers' shares were to be compared to the top five European retailers' shares, then it would become quite clear that the former is still far more concentrated than the latter.

I particularly question whether it is appropriate to describe the relationship between manufacturer and retailer as a 'balance of power'. It suggests a zero sum relationship where 'the retailer's gain is the manufacturer's loss'. This wholly misrepresents the reality, which is that both parties invest and co-operate to add value to the food marketing chain.

Concentration on own brand supply creates exactly the same dependence for the retailer as it does for any manufacturer since the retailer will lose vital supply efficiencies if sourcing of product switches too often. On the face of it, it may be thought that a larger retailer has considerable buying power and that all it has to do is move its business regularly to obtain the best price. In reality, the position is nothing like this. The proportion of own brand supply contracts which actually change hands is extremely small. I doubt whether Tesco switches as much as five per cent in an entire year. The reason for this stability is that the food chain is highly integrated. Tremendous productivity economies will have been obtained in the manufacture, distribution and marketing of own brand products by integrating the various functions of the own brand producer and the retailer. To sever a relationship with one supplier and to recreate the same level of integration with another is a wasteful, expensive and very time-consuming process.

The Tesco Story

Tesco is one of Britain's most successful food retailers. It has a market capitalisation approaching £5 billion and ranks twenty-first in the table of British companies. In 1990, it was voted the seventh best managed company in Britain in a survey organised by *The Economist* magazine. Over the last five years it has enjoyed average annual profits growth of 22 per cent. In 1991 alone, Tesco invested almost £1 billion in new stores and new technology.

All this is in stark contrast to the situation just over ten years ago when the company was in severe difficulty. At that time it had a market capitalisation of just £200 million, low profit margins (2 per cent of sales), 700 small and increasingly old-fashioned retail outlets and little or no capital investment. Indeed, ten years ago the company was ripe for takeover and there is an apocryphal tale which relates that a major multinational company did actually consider buying Tesco but ultimately rejected the idea because Tesco's image was felt to be too down market and would reflect badly on the group's existing businesses!

Yet in the 1950s and 1960s Tesco had been enormously successful and the rise, fall and rise again of the Tesco brand is all the more remarkable since the brand name itself never changed despite endorsing at least three different brand positionings. The development of the Tesco brand provides, in my view, some useful insights into the real nature of retail branding.

The 'first' Tesco brand was created by its founder, Jack Cohen. He started out in the 1920s with a market stall in the East End of London trading cheap job lots. The business enjoyed rapid expansion in the booming post-war years due, in large measure, to the benefits of converting his stores to a self-service format. In the early 1960s Jack Cohen and his company were instrumental in bringing about the abolition of Resale Price Maintenance (a practice which allowed manufacturers legally to enforce resale prices for their products, thereby effectively stifling retail price competition). This practice was abolished by Parliament in 1964 and thereafter Tesco became firmly established as the UK's leading price discount brand. Rapid expansion followed, much of it through acquisition, and during this period the company adopted trading stamps as an additional incentive to win customers. During the 1960s Tesco's turnover increased tenfold, a performance built on the success of its price-oriented brand proposition.

Tesco's decline started to become apparent in the 1970s. Jack Cohen had relinquished control and his successors could not sustain his clear formula nor develop any viable alternative of their own. Trading stamps became an expensive fixed overhead which, in the end, diminished rather than enhanced the company's price competitiveness.

The company expanded into non-food retailing but this served in the main to divert scarce resources away from the core business – investing in non-core activities meant that there was no money left over to invest in new stores or technology. Consequently the company found itself languishing in the high street with hundreds of small, poorly managed stores which were not only no longer cheap but were also acquiring a reputation for poor quality and bad service.

Worse still, two very clear competitive formats had emerged. The first, exemplified by Sainsbury, was a tightly controlled, highly branded business with modern supermarkets selling food of consistent good quality. The second, exemplified by Asda, was a chain of large out-of-town food and non-food stores with wide choice and very low prices. Tesco was left in the middle with a weak, outdated business format and a poor brand image.

Towards the end of the 1970s a new generation of managers led by Ian MacLaurin took control of the business. They could see that the Tesco brand in its existing state was a spent force and that an entirely new brand positioning had to be developed. Having analysed the market and the competition in detail, they decided to move Tesco's image upmarket. In addition they determined to invest in an entirely new chain of out-of-town food superstores and to close the majority of the company's existing stores.

This strategy seemed at the time to be fraught with risk given Tesco's downmarket image and its reliance on the high street, but several factors worked in its favour. First, most of the old high street property was freehold which, when sold, released property profits which could be used to fund the out-of-town expansion programme. Secondly, after the 1979–1981 recession the British economy experienced an unusually long period of stable growth and low inflation, which created a favourable climate for the slow process of 'adding-value' to the brand through gradual and incremental improvements in quality. Thirdly, the success of Sainsbury and of Marks & Spencer demonstrated that customers would choose quality over price provided that the quality offer consistently represented good overall value. Fourthly, the difficulties of

Illustration 7.6
One of Tesco's new superstores. Tesco has constructed nearly 200 of these large out-of-town superstores in the last ten years.

obtaining planning permission in the UK had meant that growth in out-of-town stores had been relatively slow. Thus, even though Tesco was late into the race it could still catch up. And fifthly, investment in computerisation enabled companies to create vastly improved efficiencies in logistics, administration, marketing and financial and management control.

Today, Tesco is a very different proposition from ten years ago. A decade of format and brand evolution, the construction of nearly 200 new stores, the closure of smaller, outdated stores, improvements in service, and the high quality of Tesco's products and of the stores themselves have all contributed to create a retail power brand.

Although the format and brand proposition can be changed over time through investment in resource and capital, it is quite a different matter to change consumer perceptions. Retail brands are highly visible and convey strong images to

Illustration 7.7

The services of the comedian, Dudley Moore, have been enlisted to promote the Tesco brand on UK television. Image advertising for all retailers is an important element of the brand mix.

consumers. If the image is unfavourable it is no easy task to change it. Our experience has shown that it can take ten years or more for customer perceptions to change. Tesco's new brand positioning was developed over ten years ago but it has taken all that time to narrow the 'perception gap'. Image advertising has been used to accelerate the process – we have enlisted the services of Dudley Moore, the well-known film actor, to promote the quality of the Tesco brand.

In this chapter I have touched on various aspects of retail branding. It is clear that retail brands are, by now, a familiar part of the landscape. Indeed, any survey of brands among British consumers will always find well-known retail brands on a level with fast moving consumer goods brands in terms of familiarity and esteem. As yet there are not many examples of international retail brands – it will be intriguing to see whether retail brands can become as international as their consumer product counterparts in the years ahead.

FROM BULK TO BRAND 8

Nicolò Polla
Marketing Director
GALBANI

The Commodity Product

Commodity products are those 'essential' goods which are part of the consumer's everyday life. They are the sort of purchase that consumers take entirely for granted. Milk, fruit, pasta, water, bread and petrol are all examples of commodity products. Such products are characterised by the fact that they are used very frequently yet have very little image or personality. Commodity products also tend to be priced extremely competitively.

In general, commodity products play a rôle in the market when the following three factors apply.

1. Where there is little product differentiation between products in the same category

Lack of product differentiation may come about because the raw materials used in the manufacturing process are very similar or because the manufacturing process does not vary from manufacturer to manufacturer. Staple foods such as milk and pasta are made by a very simple process. Because the methods involved in making such products are well-known and reasonably straightforward, there is little scope for developing a 'better product quality' proposition. Product differentiation can also be hampered by what might be termed 'the cooking effect'. As an example, products like oil,

137

butter and salt are normally combined with other ingredients and used to assist in the cooking and enriching of other foods. It is difficult for the consumer to appreciate any significant difference in the flavour of the commodity product itself when it is being used as only one small part of a complex recipe.

2. Where consumers have historically become attuned to certain items being treated as commodity products

These are products which for decades have formed part of consumers' daily life. They are easily found, cheap and are used by everyone every day. Consumers have a clear idea of what is and what is not a commodity product. In many European countries (such as Italy and France) pasta and rice have a commodity status. In other countries (like the UK) pasta is still regarded as something of a novelty and would not feature as part of the everyday diet. Once consumers have got used to the idea that a product is really a commodity it becomes very difficult to convince them otherwise.

3. Where legal restrictions exist

Some commodity products which are deemed to be essential to everyday living are controlled quite closely by the state. This is in order to protect consumers from unscrupulous profiteering on the part of manufacturers. But controls over such goods, particularly on price, can reduce competitiveness and dissuade manufacturers from making the effort to improve quality. Commodity products under these circumstances can become undifferentiated, dull, uninteresting and devoid of personality. The consumer's perception that commodity products have no specific identity is reinforced.

The Difficulties Involved in Branding Commodity Goods

Branding is of critical importance in the marketing of all products in all market categories. Through branding manufacturers add value to their products, building advantages over competitors. Branding endows a product with a specific and more distinctive identity, producing two main benefits. First, manufacturers with a strong branded product portfolio can build powerful relationships with the all-important retailer, since the latter is forced to stock strong brands to meet demand from his own customers. Brands create a kind of 'direct' relationship with the consumer in this way and this enables the manufacturer to improve his bargaining position considerably *vis-à-vis* the retailer. Secondly, by maintaining the presence of strong brands within a market, manufacturers can dissuade competitors from entering the market. The investment required on the part of such would-be competitors to attack well-established brands is very high, and often has little or no chance of success. Building strong brands enables manufacturers to preserve their position in the market and improve the security of their volumes and profits.

Branding is also important from the perspective of the retail trade and of the consumer. For the trade, the presence of leading branded products on the shelves reflects the quality of the store and its product selection expertise. For consumers, branding provides a guarantee of high quality and reliability and assists greatly in the decision-making process.

Branding commodity products is, however, a very difficult task and has a high degree of risk attached. Consumers tend to see these products as categories rather than as specific brands, and any attempt to create differentiation through branding can jeopardise the credibility of the product altogether. Building a branded commodity costs a significant amount of money and there is no guarantee of seeing any return on the investment. Because of the intrinsic characteristics of commodity based products it may prove virtually impossible, regardless of how much money is spent, to change deeply entrenched consumer attitudes. Investment in brand building and in advertising commodity products is therefore limited. Price and easy availability remain the key factors driving consumer choice between different commodity products.

However, in the last few years and despite the difficulties and risks involved, some manufacturers have started working on ways in which to differentiate their commodity products through branding. This development has come about through the realisation that the only way to build market share is to develop meaningful and specific competitive advantages which set your products apart from the rest.

Most effort has been put into the development of a differentiated *service* offer to support the commodity product. This seems to be one of the easiest ways to generate differences between products. The best example of this is the petrol industry where manufacturers have tried to add value to their product by 'branding the service'. Petrol companies have invested hundreds of millions of dollars in building powerful retail brand franchises. BP's recent international rebranding programme is a case in point. Today's service station forecourts are designed with the consumer very much in mind. Ease of access, a variety of payment options, petrol credit cards, free check-ups, car-wash facilities, shops stocking car accessory and maintenance products – all of these and more are initiatives introduced to attempt to win the consumer's loyalty to a particular branded offer. The latest development in service stations is the establishment of fully-stocked supermarket/convenience stores where consumers can buy a wide range of goods not necessarily related to the car at all.

Another important opportunity for differentiation is *packaging*, particularly in the food area. Many manufacturers have used different or functionally improved packaging as a way of offering a better alternative to customers and consumers. Examples are the one-portion butter pats sold to hotels and tinned fruits which can be used in out-of-season periods. Putting more product and nutritional information on packs and introducing more environmentally friendly packaging can also help in this regard.

Finally, above and below-the-line *support and promotion* has been used to communicate the different rational and emotional properties of certain commodity products. One of the best examples of this is the banana branded Chiquita, which today, after years of investment in advertising, has a powerful image as a high quality banana product. The International Wool Secretariat has developed, through the ubiquitous 'Woolmark', a powerful brand recognised by consumers around the world as a guarantee of the origin and quality of the wool content of the garment or product it endorses.

The process of branding commodity products is still in its infancy, but there are clear signals that it is becoming an important means of remaining competitive.

The European Cheese Market

Cheese is a food which is very close to being a commodity product. Its qualities make it almost a dietary essential and it has a high level of everyday family use in many countries across Europe. Cheese is also a fresh product which means that it must be consumed quickly.

Cheese is made in a wide variety of geographical areas, each of which has its own cheese-making culture and approach. Some cheese-making communities focus on the manufacture of localised or regional cheeses whereas others focus on national cheeses.

All of these factors have to date hampered the development of brands in the European cheese market. All cheeses in particular market segments (for example, variants of mozzarella, brie, cheddar or provolone) continue to be seen as representative of the segment overall, rather than as having their own identity. Nevertheless, the European cheese market has seen a significant boost in the development of brands over the last ten years. There are three main reasons for this.

Trade concentration

The rapid expansion of large self-service retail stores, where the requirement to attract a consumer's attention is paramount, has meant that cheese has had to become more visibly branded. Manufacturers have had to provide a wider range of more innovative products. These products have two sets of values:

(i)   'real' or functional values such as ease of use, size, range, and so on

(ii)   'emotional' values of image, reliability, awareness

The need to introduce these innovations has forced manufacturers both to improve the quality and appearance of their products and to market them under a brand name, in order to win the consumer's loyalty and trust in this highly competitive environment.

The innovation rate has been lower in countries such as Italy, where the advent of the superstore and of modern distribution techniques are less in evidence. In countries like Italy, most stores still offer a selection of uncut, unbranded products whose merits are promoted by the retailers themselves. Thus retailers are seen by the consumer as being highly reliable advisers.

Consumer demand for higher quality

Increased consumer demand for better quality products has encouraged the development of higher standards in the presentation and preparation of fresh foods. This is a major consumer trend in most food markets. The widespread interest in healthy eating coupled with a desire for a better standard of living has led to people eating less food but of a much higher quality. To answer this growing need, many manufacturers have started to raise the quality of their products in order to make them stand out in the market. They have also started to brand their products and advertise them to the trade and consumers in order to promote their products' superiority.

Growth of multinational companies

The growth of multinational companies, whose strategic orientation is to develop international brands suitable for all markets, has focused attention on how to achieve this aim with commodity products like cheese. 'International' products can be highly profitable because of the large volumes they provide and the consequent savings that can be achieved on investment in R & D, production and media.

These three factors have had a more noticeable impact on the cheese market in northern Europe where more innovative product development and more visibly 'branded' markets have developed. By contrast, most southern European countries have maintained a strong local cheese tradition but have seen a very low response to the need to innovate.

The Italian Cheese Market

The Italian cheese market is the second largest in Europe after France, producing 1 000 000 tonnes per annum in volume – equivalent to about $8 billion at retail value. The market is divided into two sections, 'fresh products' and 'seasoned products', which respectively make up 35 per cent and 65 per cent of the total market. The main characteristics of the Italian cheese market are its strong traditions and the fact that branding, at least to date, has been quite limited. Within the Italian cheese market the following key factors prevail.

Tradition

Cheese is a food which has strong links to the historical traditions of the country. The reasons for this include: its heritage – cheese was first produced in Italy many centuries ago; and its rural origins – cheese was originally hand-made in areas such as the mountains in the north and the valleys in the south where there was a natural abundance of cow and buffalo milk. The first cheese manufacturers built their factories close to these areas of milk production in order to limit manufacturing costs and avoid the problems involved in transporting milk over long distances. This emphasis on local production has reinforced the consumer's perception of cheese as a locally produced, fresh, high quality food. This perception still exists today despite the fact that many factories these days are located far from the source of milk production. The consumer's perception of cheese as a fresh, high quality product is a reflection of the Italian cheese manufacturers' continued focus on quality of raw materials and the hygienic nature of the manufacturing process as well as an enduring respect for the traditional methods of production.

A different cultural significance

The relationship between cheese and consumers in Italy is different from that in other countries such as France. French consumers regard cheese as a complex food, in which milk is just one ingredient. Italian consumers consider cheese to be a simple and natural raw material. To them, cheese is just another way of consuming milk. In France, cheese has always been regarded as a more élitist food, due to its popularity with the upper classes. As a result, there are more strong-tasting, elaborate cheeses in France. These are suitable for gastronomic consumption (a cheese board is always available at restaurants) and targeted at connoisseurs. In Italy cheese is regarded as a more natural food, with closer links to rural culture and the traditions of local manufacture. It tends to have a more gentle, milky taste, which encourages daily family consumption.

Low presence of brands

Branded products represent less than 40 per cent of the total cheese market in Italy and the development of 'branded cheeses' has been restricted by three factors:

(i) The perception of cheese as a natural fresh product encourages consumers to buy locally-made, unpackaged cheeses.

(ii)   The nature of the products is such that they appear in well-known and traditional flavours, shapes and sizes. Consumers are less inclined to accept change. This limits manufacturers' opportunities for product differentiation, a key variable in the development of competitive brands.

(iii) The fragmented nature of the Italian distribution system and the lack of any major multiple retail system means that it is difficult to get branded cheese to the consumer. Traditional small independent retailers, who still hold more than 60 per cent of the total cheese business, prefer unbranded products which in this environment allow higher margins than their branded equivalents.

Galbani

It is truly remarkable therefore that, against this apparently unpromising background, one brand, Galbani, has grown to be the largest branded cheese manufacturer in Italy and indeed in the world (see Plates 14–21 for examples of Galbani's cheese portfolio). Galbani is used both as a range or 'umbrella' name to endorse a variety of proprietary product brands like Bel Paese, Santa Lucia and Certosa, and as a brand name in its own right to distinguish one generic type of cheese, such as provolone or gorgonzola, from another. The relevance of the Galbani endorsement to the product-led brands varies according to the individual strengths of the sub-brands. In the case of a strong brand like Bel Paese, for instance, it could be argued that the brand would do just as well without the Galbani endorsement if all other elements of the brand personality were left intact. But with other product brands such as Santa Lucia and Certosa, the interdependency of the product-led brand and the umbrella brand is more in evidence.

Galbani is a powerful national brand name. Since its beginnings at the end of the nineteenth century, Galbani has always produced high quality products which follow the Italian cheese tradition. Galbani produces all kinds of Italian cheese, from fresh products (mozzarella, ricotta, crescenza) to matured products (gorgonzola, provolone – see Plate 17). Galbani has over the years become an integral part of the Italian way of life.

Galbani has the image of original and genuine Italian cheese and its success in creating a powerful brand out of a commodity product can be put down to the following factors.

A high level of product quality

Product quality is achieved through the use of carefully selected raw materials and ingredients, adherence to traditional production processes and rigorous quality control techniques. Though cheese is high in fat, it does not appear to have suffered from the shift in consumer tastes towards healthier food products. Indeed Galbani seems, if anything, to have benefited from its image as a natural and unprocessed cheese.

Galbani products compare favourably to those of small, local manufacturers and provide a level of consistency, both from product to product and over time, that others would find hard to rival. The fact that in cheeses Galbani has remained true to its heritage and produced only cheeses which are perceived as traditional and Italian further underlines the brand's stability.

A strong consumer franchise

Galbani commands significant brand awareness brought about largely as a result of a massive investment in advertising throughout the 1960s and early 1970s. Galbani was positioned as a high quality, reliable cheese producer. The advertising strapline to back up this proposition '*Galbani Vuol Dire Fiducia*' (that is, 'Galbani Means Trustworthiness') has become one of the most well known in Italy. In the absence of a national Italian Cheese Board overseas importers look to Galbani to provide a reference for Italian cheese. During the 1980s most of the advertising behind the brand was withdrawn, yet the consumer franchise that had been created remained in place. Italian consumers have clearly taken the Galbani brand personality to their hearts.

Indeed, figures for brand awareness would lead one to believe that the Galbani brand has continued to be well supported over the past ten years. 73 per cent of Italian consumers, when asked to name a brand of cheese, cite Galbani whereas competitor brands achieve awareness ratings of significantly less then 50 per cent. Prompted awareness of Galbani is virtually 100 per cent.

Advertising is not, however, the only reason for Galbani's high consumer awareness. Galbani's brand personality is communicated to its audiences through a variety of other means, including:

(i) a powerful visual identity which dominates most super-market shelves

(ii) the influence of small retailers (the traditional outlet for bulk cheese sales) who unpack and sell Galbani products by the piece

(iii) Galbani delivery vans (*camioncini*) all of which are painted with the famous red and white Galbani logo and each week visit virtually every city and village in the country distributing Galbani products

Since the acquisition of the Galbani company by BSN in 1989 it has been agreed that significant investment should be put behind the brand to secure its franchise more effectively through increased levels of advertising spend. This will serve to consolidate the brand's strength.

Strong distribution

The Galbani delivery system is the largest in Europe. From its factories around Italy, Galbani delivers its products in its own trucks to 140 depots, and from there deliveries are made in Galbani painted *camioncini* to around 230 000 outlets across the country on a daily basis. The majority of these outlets are small independent stores or delicatessens specialising in cheese, though deliveries are also made to hotels, restaurants and caterers. What they get from Galbani is an excellent standard of service complemented by a field force of 2000 sales representatives, a powerful competitive advantage which none of Galbani's competitors can match.

Galbani has also extended these strong links overseas. Galbani has been exporting to Germany since 1935 and to the United States since 1940. Between 1945 and 1955 the company started to export to France, Switzerland, the United Kingdom and Belgium. In the United States, Belgium, Switzerland and the UK Galbani directly owns the companies which import and market its cheeses, thereby keeping close control over the distribution chain. In France and Germany Galbani uses a powerful independent distribution arrangement.

Competitive pricing

Galbani is a mass producer of cheese and related products and can achieve significant economies of scale. As a result Galbani products are priced very competitively.

✳   ✳   ✳

These four factors (product quality, strong consumer franchise, powerful distribution and competitive pricing) have helped to build Galbani's reputation as a reliable company. Galbani is seen as *the* premier Italian cheese company and the second largest company in food overall. Consumers trust Galbani because it produces good, fresh cheeses at honest prices. However, the market environment is changing very quickly and Galbani will need to react fast if it is to stay ahead. The major factors which Galbani will need to address are as follows:

Distribution

The Italian distribution system is steadily evolving towards a more modern format, with large retail multiples growing in size and importance. Since these multiple retailers have their own wholesaling and distribution systems, the competitive edge held by Galbani by virtue of its distribution power will be eroded. Such large retailers will also seek other manufacturers' products.

In markets such as the UK and France, the power of the retailers is such that they source and sell products which carry the retailer's own name (these are known as 'own label' products or 'own brands'). Such own label products may be supplied by any number of manufacturers and often replace the lesser known and cheaper brands on the shelves. The only brands which tend not to suffer from such retailer power are the number one and number two brands in the market. These top brands are not only strong enough to sell alongside own label products, but are a *sine qua non* for retailers who profess to offer customers a full range of groceries. Ironically therefore, Galbani could actually benefit from a shift in retail power to the multiples. Galbani, after all, is the name that consumers will be looking for when scanning the shelves, so the retailer (even one with significant buying power) cannot afford not to stock Galbani products.

However, only a minority of Galbani products are sold in prepackaged form. The majority are sold at the delicatessen counter and are sliced from larger cheeses and sold in plain or 'retailer' wrapping. Moreover, because these products are sold to the consumer without any packaging or visual identity, it is difficult for the consumer to know what brand of cheese is being bought. Hence, for these delicatessen products it is relatively easy for the retailer to switch to manufacturers who can provide the required quality but at the most competitive price.

Innovation

Consumers are increasingly seeking higher levels of service and more innovative products. New product development therefore forms an integral part of the strategy to keep the Galbani brand young and up to date. A top quality, traditionally made mozzarella has, for example, been launched under the name Vallelatte. There are also plans to introduce a range of low fat cheeses, though it is recognised that such an introduction should be handled very carefully and sensitively. Overall, however, though such developments are important, they should not detract from the need to develop the core brand personality. Galbani has recognised the significance of product branding and the importance of the Galbani endorsement. It is this recognition that has prompted the recent change in advertising policy. Any development or contemporisation of the Galbani brand image must obviously be handled sensitively and must take into account the powerful perceptions and preconceptions that consumers already have about the brand.

Competition

Competition is increasing between manufacturers, all of whom want to increase share in what are essentially very mature markets. The cheese market is also very fragmented. Galbani, Invernizzi and Locatelli offer a full range of Italian cheeses, whereas Kraft only offers processed 'American' cheese. In addition, there are other brand names which are known throughout Italy, though only for certain types of cheeses. Then there are a host of local cheese makers, selling only through local outlets. Clearly this fragmentation gives Galbani an advantage, since none of Galbani's competitors can offer as full a range of products or as comprehensive a national coverage as Galbani.

*   *   *

The challenge for Galbani is to ensure that the powerful equity of the Galbani brand is reinforced and maintained. Changes are forcing Galbani to develop additional areas of strength in order to stay competitive and to continue to grow. Galbani's objectives for the future reflect the philosophy of its new owner, BSN, one of Europe's leading branded goods manufacturers: focus more on the consumer, add value in all areas of the marketing mix and build on a successful history.

FRANCHISING: HOW BRAND POWER WORKS 9

Luciano Benetton
President
BENETTON

It is perhaps a little curious that I have been asked to write about the relation of brand power to franchising as the Benetton brand (see Plates section) has never been developed as a franchising operation and there are no plans to do so in the future. However, as our distribution system is similar in important respects to franchising, and as both approaches reward the entrepreneurial drive of individual proprietors, I feel comfortable discussing the relative merits of each. In addition, I will explain how our distribution system became an integral part of the global enterprise that is Benetton today.

What is Franchising?

The term franchising comes from the French word meaning 'free from servitude'. The original meaning still has some relevance since, in contemporary terms, franchisees are 'free' to own their own businesses even if they lack the requisite commercial experience and have only limited capital.

The US Department of Commerce in its *Franchise Opportunities Handbook* describes franchising as

a form of licensing by which the owner, or franchisor, of a product, service or method obtains distribution through

151

affiliated dealers or franchisees. The product, method or service being marketed is identified by a brand name and the franchisor maintains control over the marketing methods employed. In many cases the operation is like a large chain, with trade marks, uniform symbols, equipment, storefronts and standardised services or products and maintains practices as outlined in the franchise agreement.

A similar definition is offered by the International Franchise Association:

A continuing relationship in which the franchisor provides a licensed privilege to do business, plus assistance in organising, training, merchandising and management in return for a (financial) consideration from the franchisee.

Another observer put it even more succinctly:

A system where, in reward for payment, you allow another person to copy your successful business in every respect.

The precise origins of franchising are unclear. According to one theory, franchising was first developed in the late 1920s by a French wool producer, Roubaix, which was trying to establish a strong distribution chain for its products. It set up a chain of stores specialising in selling knitting wool, called the 'Wool of Penguin'. The chain of independent stores was linked to Roubaix by a contract which gave each store owner exclusive use of the trade mark (supported by advertising) in a particular, well-defined territory. This relationship between independent shop and producer was not yet called franchising, but it had all the key characteristics.

Meanwhile, a similar development was taking place in the USA, although the reasons for it were quite different. At the beginning of the 1930s the US auto industry was confronted by a barrage of anti-trust legislation which forbade any form of vertical integration. US auto manufacturers were therefore unable to control the supply of fuel to car owners. To get round this, General Motors developed a form of contract that linked the retailer of fuel and petrol to the parent company in a less direct way. These contracts represented the first steps in the USA towards developing the concept of franchising contracts.

Whatever the difficulties in precisely defining franchising or tracing its origins, it is relatively easy to identify its characteristics and critical components. The main elements provided by franchisors to franchisees are, according to most lawyers and academics, the following:

— A piece of intellectual property, rights over which are protected by license

— Good commercial methods, systems or procedures

— Training

— Assistance with site location

— Territorial exclusivity

— Precise rules as to termination/renewal/the basis of the agreement (a contract of fixed duration which includes an option for renewal is standard).

— Suggested selling prices (whether or not a franchisor can impose a selling price on a franchisee depends on the country where the store is located; mostly strict maintenance of retail prices is illegal)

In return for such a 'package' of rights and benefits franchisees pay a fee to the franchisor.

Similarities between Franchising and Benetton's System

Although Benetton has never been in the franchising business, some of the fundamental concepts of franchising are integral to the relationship we seek to establish with our independent store-owners. Among the elements we provide are:

(i)   A protected trade mark

(ii)   An original and exclusive range of products, services and trading procedures

(iii)   A healthy profit motivation

(iv)   A certain amount of commercial expertise

Trade Marks

Trade mark rights have always been important to Benetton, long before we could envisage any real international success. The very first sweaters sold by the Benetton family back in 1955 were branded under the *Trés Jolie* name, a name which at the time we did not bother to register. We also chose something French because in those days France represented the height of fashion to Italians. And when in 1964 we opened our first shop in Belluno, Italy, we picked an English name, *My Market* as it was then the era of Carnaby Street and Swinging London and English names brought that far-off youth revolution closer to Italy.

A year later we opened our first factory in Ponzano, Treviso, and our second store in the exclusive ski resort of Cortina D'Ampezzo. This store was also called *My Market*, but we decided to label the products Benetton, using white letters on a bright green background with the symbol of a knitting knot in graphic form. This label has evolved over time, but it is still the basis of our corporate identity today (Plate 22).

As brand names and symbols became increasingly popular during the 1970s, we paid more attention to this aspect of our business. For example, we bought the name *Sisley* from its French owner in 1970, the only name we acquired and then developed; all the others we developed from scratch. We also registered a variety of store names in the 1970s and 1980s – *My Market, Tomato, Jeans West, Merceria* and *Fantomax* – as well as a number of product brand names – *012 Benetton, Zerotondo, Kix 712, Giuliana Benetton for Shoes,* and so on.

Over all this time, we have never underestimated the importance of our trade marks. We protect them rigorously, even in areas noted for piracy such as South America and the Far East, and we are extremely scrupulous about licensing out our name – any potential licensees must adhere to strict quality standards.

An original and exclusive product range

This is guaranteed by the fact that independent shop owners only sell our products in their shops, and we only supply such outlets. In the early days of our business our clothes were a novelty in themselves. Knitwear at that time was a marginal part of the average Italian wardrobe. Conservatively designed and coloured, it was priced at the higher end of the market and worn mostly by older people. Because my sister Giuliana and I were teenagers, we naturally addressed ourselves to customers of our own age. Our knits were brightly-coloured, accessibly priced and youthfully designed. They stood out when displayed among other products in store windows. Our first collection had just five styles – but we offered each in thirty-six colours.

We benefited, as did many Italian enterprises, from the country's economic boom in the 1960s. It was so powerful that it seemed unrepeatable and unstoppable, and encouraged many entrepreneurs to focus only on quick profit in the short term. But our market was becoming overcrowded, a phenomenon which economists refer to as 'mature'. If we wanted to survive long term, we had to concentrate on innovation and development.

We persisted with a tenacity that I think is often characteristic of Venetians. Colour was our major innovation. By developing a technique for dyeing finished garments, we expanded both the colour choice for the consumer and our ability to respond quickly to market needs.

But colour was not our only contribution to the modernisation of a 'mature' market. In 1962 I discovered a knitting machine in Scotland that made wool feel soft and cashmere-like. We were the first manufacturers to use such machines in Italy. Then in 1966, we had the opportunity to buy some outdated factory equipment. With some modifications, these machines could be used for knitting, so we bought 260. Each machine was costly, but our efforts yielded a machine worth ten times the cost price and which reduced both waste and production time.

We were also always on the look-out for ways to shorten the traditional cycle of the apparel business: production/warehousing/wholesaler/retailer. Heavy investment in technology in the 1980s has helped us reduce the stages in this cycle so that production now interfaces directly with the retailer. In 1984, for example, we completed a robotic distribution centre in Castrette, a completely automated facility that is still highly advanced even by current standards. It eliminated the two intermediate steps of our business cycle (warehousing and wholesale), shortening the time between production and customer. Our distribution centre now handles 28 000 boxes and 800 shipments in each 24-hour period. Over a 12-day cycle we ship products to every one of our 7000 stores worldwide and our turnaround speed is the envy of many industries.

The concept of the retail store is just as important, however, as that of the product, (see Plate 23). Having as a young man worked in stores in Treviso, I knew from that experience exactly what I did not want our stores to look like. I did not, for example, want a store where counters and boxes separated the merchandise from the customer, where customers had to ask the shop clerk for permission to touch the clothes or where the atmosphere was dark and unfriendly.

In 1965 we used the name *My Market* for our first store in Belluno, not only because of its English associations, but because it suggested what we were trying to achieve with that store, and every one of our stores since – the feel of an open-air market where the customer is free to pick and choose from a variety of readily available merchandise.

I had already seen mono-product stores in Rome in 1960 and was convinced that a small store selling only one product could be more profitable than a larger, less focused outlet. When this hypothesis proved correct in Belluno, I asked architect Tobia Scarpa (with whom we had established a friendly relationship) to design the interior for the second store in Cortina D'Ampezzo a year later. This time we made a real break with tradition, eliminating the counter that separates the customer from the clothes. Instead, there was a simple table for the cash register. The small space was designed to be light and luminous and was accented with light wood so as to have a vaguely Scandinavian effect. All the colour then came from the clothes; what we sought to achieve was a European aesthetic within the American context of freedom.

The result met with widespread approval, especially from the young people who were our target customers. The store in Cortina was not only a success in itself, it also served as a showcase for the trend-setting young crowd who gathered there during the winter ski season. We realised full well that we would begin to attract the interest of competitors as well as customers but we could not compromise on a successful retail strategy because of fear of imitation. We also preferred to become even more innovative, competing with our own successful interiors, rather than worrying too much about competition.

With this in mind, we asked Scarpa to design several store interiors to appeal to different clients and varying local tastes. *Merceria* was designed with a 'classic' feel which was aimed at the mothers of our customers in *My Market*; *Tomato* was glossy, chromatic and ultramodern and Fantomax had the feel of Art Nouveau and Swinging London. This way, we effectively blanketed the Italian market over a period of ten years.

A healthy profit motivation

This is, as we noted earlier, one of the driving forces in the growth of franchising and it is an important element in our growth as well. The majority of our immediate clients, the store owners, did not have retail experience, at least in the early years, but they were sincere, highly motivated and full of energy. They all had an entrepreneurial spirit that found its expression through the Benetton network. They are proud to call themselves 'Benettonians'.

Commercial expertise

This is a further distinguishing characteristic of most franchise relationships but Benetton does *not* provide this kind of training; this is one of the major differences between our approach and that of a classic franchise system. We do not sell a package of classroom instructions; nor do we ask for any royalties on sales. However, through the representative network which we have developed over the years we communicate a lot of market expertise, and of course our technological expertise – in receiving, executing and shipping orders – benefits anyone in the Benetton network.

Freedom vs Franchising

The franchisee necessarily relinquishes some freedom of action because franchisors have to exert some degree of control over operations bearing their trade mark. Franchisors impose certain standards of quality necessary to maintain the uniformity and individuality of the service offered and it is essential to ensure that the operation of each outlet reflects favourably on the organisation as a whole. McDonald's in America is a well-known example of a franchise which applies this principle meticulously, and when we are sometimes referred to as 'the fast food of fashion' I consider it a compliment.

We learned our lesson in the importance of quality standards when we opened our first stores outside Italy. Our first international outpost was opened in Paris in 1969 and it was very successful, but from that experience we learned the importance of shop cleanliness and the proper display of clothes. Original products and an innovative interior were not enough; we had grown to the point where a certain consistency of image had to be maintained if we were to continue on the road to international expansion.

The extent of control varies as between a franchise and a related distribution system such as ours. Among the services normally provided by franchisors to franchisees are:

— Location analysis and advice

— Store development assistance, including lease negotiation

— Store design and sourcing of equipment

— Initial employee and management training and continuing management counselling

— Advertising and merchandising advice and assistance

— Standardised procedures and operations

— Centralised purchasing with consequent savings

— Financial assistance in the establishment of the business

Our system includes certain of these elements: for example, some advice on location by our representatives, suggestions on shop decor, assistance with advertising and help with product ranges, but many other aspects of our approach are uniquely Benetton – when I reflect on how we operate I realise that Benetton is an idiosyncratic blend of planning and serendipity.

The Benetton Network

We had never wanted to become directly involved in the selling phase, so in the early days friends with financial resources performed this function within our overall business concept. We selected them, however, on the basis of personal knowledge and individual capability, rather than on their commercial experience and sometimes this proved a distinct advantage. They were often more flexible and enthusiastic and could adapt more readily to a young clientele and a new concept. Some also came from prominent local families and were able to attract a following by their presence alone.

Our first few stores were financed fifty–fifty between us and the store operators, but we quickly found people willing to underwrite all the costs of opening a new store. Our system was also less formal than the US model, and because many of our clients were friends, or friends of friends, we did not ask them to give us a percentage of profits. Frankly, I was uncomfortable with the idea of American-style contracts. They were too rigid, too like the old system of merchandising or the counters which we had abolished in our stores. Without contracts or signatures we had already by the mid-1960s built a factory and opened up 300 stores in Italy and we saw no need to change.

These friends became the foundation of our representative network. They were our 'entrepreneurs of distribution'. Their rôle at first was to open, at their own cost, a point of sale and then, as the local representative, to encourage the opening of other shops in the area with whom they could establish a relationship. Our representatives also served as 'go-betweens' who conveyed important marketing information to headquarters.

However, when we began to expand internationally we modified this system. The first stores abroad, for example, were owned directly by Benetton so that we could understand at first hand the local market. We spent a lot of time in the second half of the 1970s developing foreign markets in a systematic fashion. We concentrated, for example, on prime locations for our stores and the results justified our efforts: between 1977 and 1978 foreign sales doubled, and the following year they increased sevenfold.

Today our representative network consists of 80 offices worldwide, each one responsible for a precise geographic area. Together they employ more than 800 people and these are the point of contact between Benetton and the galaxy of 7000 independent stores that sell our product. Our representatives are expected to recruit new 'Benettonians', identify potential shop sites, and liaise with the independent retailers, our customers and with headquarters in Treviso. Our two major annual fashion collections are shown to them before going into production and our representatives receive a commission on Benetton sales of clothing to the store owners in their area.

But it should be noted that unlike franchising, we receive no royalties on sales, nor any other kind of fee or compensation and nor do we concede territorial exclusivity. Our ties with our independently-owned network are based more on verbal agreements and a handshake than on contracts. It is really quite a simple equation: a Benetton shop owner agrees to sell Benetton products and, in exchange, we agree to take care of the image and promotion of the Benetton trademarks and guarantee speed and reliability in the supply of the merchandise.

How Brand Power Works

A simple, but unplanned, reason for our success is the curious phonetic quality of our name: 'Benetton' seems somewhat English to the English, French to the French, German to the Germans and so on. The roots of the name are so international that it seems it can be readily adopted in all countries and is easy to pronounce in all languages.

But our spectacular growth in only twenty-five years has not been achieved solely on the basis of a name, nor on a notion about bright colours, nor on a willingness to invest in technology and new store development. I am convinced that no idea lasts forever; you have to know how to re-invent yourself. This is true in just about any industry, but it is essential in the fast-paced world of fashion. In Benetton we have shown an ability, I believe, constantly to re-invigorate the brand so that it remains contemporary and appealing in a rapidly changing world. For example:

(i) We started out with knitwear, but now we produce a full range of 7500 styles of clothing each year.

(ii) In the beginning our apparel was strictly casual, for a specific age group. Now we offer a total look, for many ages, and with appropriate accessories.

(iii) From one designer, Giuliana, in our earliest years, we now have 200 people in the company who plan 7500 styles each year.

(iv) Our stores were intentionally small at first, a total of perhaps 50–60 square metres. As our offer has increased, we increased the size of some stores, especially in the US market.

(v) In our first years of international expansion we distributed the same models to every country, refusing requests to modify according to local needs. Now we set the overall fashion themes, while each individual store owner has some latitude to order on the basis of local tastes.

(vi) From one factory in Italy in 1965, we now operate fourteen factories in eight countries serving 7000 points of sale in 100 countries. We also have 16 licensing agreements in twenty-eight countries for the use of the Benetton trade mark in the production of clothing. In addition there are thirty international licenses for a variety of other items including cosmetics, toys, bathing suits, eyewear, watches, stationery, undergarments and shoes.

(vii) Like many Italian companies that flourished in the boom years of the 1960s we were originally a traditional, family-owned business, but to achieve global dimensions, we took on professional management and a corporate structure. We are now listed on the stock exchanges of Milan, Frankfurt, London, New York and Toronto.

We also saw the risk of weakening and diluting our image as we diversified and expanded internationally so, during the 1980s, we deliberately narrowed our communications focus to support only a few trademarks: *United Colors of Benetton, Sisley* and *012 Benetton*.

Advertising has always been important to us as a way of strengthening and focusing our brand image. In 1981 we launched our first worldwide campaign specifically aimed at reinforcing brand recognition and this marked the beginning of our collaboration with Oliviero Toscani and the French advertising agency, Eldorado. The resulting campaign, 'All the colours of the world', showed multiracial groups of young people jumping and laughing. It attracted immediate attention, some of it controversial.

This multiracial theme was repeated in succeeding years with the slogan 'United Colors of Benetton', a slogan so successful that it became the trade mark of the company. United Colors of Benetton is rich with meaning; it suggests among other things the United States, united races, a united

Europe and a united world. This is consistent with the philosophy of our company, which is truly global and generates the majority of its revenues and profits outside Italy.

Our advertising is now frequently dedicated to social themes such as war, over-population, equality, AIDS, and the environment; important social themes such as these constitute a unifying element for all our communications (see Plates section for examples of Benetton advertising). Our billboards decorate the urban environment in every country of the world and we use them to promote images intended to overcome indifference and apathy. They are meant to draw attention, and they succeed in doing so – sometimes more than we had planned. 1989 for example was the year of our campaign for equality. One of our advertisements portrayed two men, one black and one white, handcuffed together; another portrayed a black mother nursing a white baby and the clothes they were wearing had only symbolic value (Plate 27). The campaign caused a sensation in the USA but it received awards in many European countries.

In 1991, we ran a picture of a war cemetery which provoked controversy in the heat of the Gulf conflict; our objective was to show that war is a terrible thing (Plate 26). And our multicoloured prophylactics generated lively debate; here we wanted to highlight the importance of preventive measures against AIDS. Finally, a graphic photo of a newborn baby caused a great deal of controversy; our intent in this instance was to pay homage to life – we hoped that the baby would remind us that we all begin the same way and that differences are instilled only after birth.

We pay great attention to our advertising and to all our corporate communications. The themes we touch on are socially-orientated and universal because we are speaking to audiences in 100 different countries. When we succeed in provoking thought and breaking through barriers of indifference in myriad cultures and continents our objective has been reached.

The Benetton Group today invests 4 per cent of sales in communication. We are present in 300 magazines, 70 000 billboards, 40 000 posters in our outlets and 5 million catalogues. In late 1991, we began to publish and distribute worldwide one million copies of a new magazine, *Colors*, produced in five languages. It is available in all our stores and sold on selected newstands. It discusses themes relating to culture and the environment in various countries of the world.

A global company should, however, reinforce its image through a variety of communications media and not just through advertising. Sponsorship is one such medium and Benetton owns and directs its own Formula One motor racing team (see Plate 29). All the characteristics of Grand Prix racing – speed, colour, internationality, excitement, plus the irresistible combination of high technology and the human factor – are a perfect expression of our corporate philosophy. This affiliation has been effective in creating an image for us in a number of countries even *before* we have established a commercial presence. It is also an important showcase as Grand Prix racing is a sporting event that continues, through trials and official races, eleven months of the year, year after year, and it is truly a world spectacle, with sixteen Grand Prix races on four continents, viewed by a television audience estimated at 4 billion in over sixty countries.

In addition, we are active in the sponsorship of basketball, volleyball and rugby (Plate 30), based on the conviction that sport is important to everyone and especially to young people. Sport is a metaphor for dynamism, loyalty, competition and colour, all of which Benetton represents.

Final Thoughts

It has been said that brands in the fashion sector begin as the passion of one person and often lose their way when that one person is gone. The enduring brands are those which are able to substitute the cult of personality for a more universal and communicable set of values through a network of individuals.

I have always insisted that the foundation for everything Benetton has become is our people. The growth we have experienced would be unthinkable without the co-operation of Benetton store owners and staff, our network of representatives, the creative thinkers inside the company – indeed, the energy of all our employees.

We have also learned to communicate our underlying values in every expression of our corporate being, from the design of our stores to the layout of our factories, from our reliance on technology to our emphasis on handshakes. The Benetton rainbow today arches far above the dreams of three brothers and a sister in post-war Italy. Yet I believe that the humanity of our origins shines through in everything we do.

PROTECTING POWER BRANDS 10

Garo Partoyan
MARS INCORPORATED

The strategy had been right and the execution perfect; sufficient resources and time had also been committed and the result was a *power brand*, a unique asset whose profitability would generate funds sufficient not only to sustain the brand's leadership position but also to support and finance other aspects of the business. The brand was number one in its sector, had a high level of awareness, an unequivocal and distinctive brand image, and it offered benefits and qualities readily understood and appreciated by a loyal consumer base. In short, a powerful brand franchise had been created, something of great value.

But this, on its own, is not enough. A true power brand must have all of the characteristics set out above but it must also be protected at law as a trade mark.

The unique characteristics of the brand must of course be preserved. This vital task is normally carried out by the marketing experts. But it is equally important to ensure that the brand be protected in legal terms. Third parties, for example, must not be allowed to encroach upon the brand's franchise; they must be kept at a clear distance and prevented from taking advantage of its goodwill and reputation. Such protection is necessary not only to keep competitors from riding on the power brand's coat tails but also to ensure that there is no dilution or whittling away of the range and breadth of legal protection to which the power brand is entitled.

167

The Process

There are many ways to ensure that a power brand is legally protected. Registering the brand name and other distinctive elements of the brand presentation as trade marks[1], securing copyright in graphic aspects of the brand presentation and advertising, searching actively in the marketplace for possible infringements, and acting aggressively to stop activities of others that take advantage of the brand franchise (that is, that threaten the power brand owner's exclusive rights) – all these activities help to protect a brand's legal rights.

When should these things be done? The answer is that it is never too soon to take steps to protect a brand's legal rights. Indeed, many protective measures should be initiated at the outset of a brand's life; but it is never too late to start protecting the brand actively or increasing the level of activity in the brand protection area. The important point is that comprehensive protection of a power brand requires an active, continuous and well thought out programme that anticipates problems, is flexible enough to be responsive to a variety of situations, and which can quickly provide a robust and convincing response when problems arise.

Competent trade mark legal and litigation counsel should be appointed in each country of significance where the power brand is sold. Counsel should be familiar with the brand and its franchise as well as with the business and personnel involved in managing the brand so that, when the need arises for prompt and effective action, time is not lost and information about the threatening activity can be efficiently assimilated by counsel. This sort of preparation is further strengthened by having comprehensive evidence of use on the brand, based on sales, geographic distribution of such sales and evidence from advertising records, as well as affidavits and other documents, so that information relevant to the issues of the conflict can be readily presented. Ideally, such evidence should be maintained in a reasonable state-of-readiness so that it can quickly be updated, completed and used.

The Importance of Trade Marks

Probably the most important aspect of any protection programme is the maintenance and protection of registered trade marks. Obviously, the brand name itself is usually the single most distinctive element of a brand and this should be registered in the form of simple block letters or in pictograms of the relevant language or languages. For example M&M's, a brand of chocolate candies, is one of my company's most valuable power brands (Plate 31). The name is registered in simple block letters but also in any stylised or fanciful forms in which it is customarily used, for example when used in conjunction with candies (see below). Where any such 'logo' form of the trade mark has special colours, the mark is registered in black and white as well as in a form where those colours are specifically designated as part of the registration. We have found that such an approach is especially useful in situations where an encroacher's trade mark and/or style differs from our own but where their colour combination is closely similar to that of our power brand. For example, Tantine for rice was stopped in France because the styling of

Illustration 10.1
M&M's is one of the most valuable power brands owned by Mars.

the letters and the colours were found to be confusingly similar to those of our own Uncle Ben's rice brand.

What about designs or so-called 'devices'? My advice is that the owner should register them. Indeed, if the design or device (that is, the logo) is an important symbol of the brand as with the Mercedes-Benz star, or the Apple Computer apple, or the Woolmark device or the Shell Oil stylised shell, registration is essential.

Illustration 10.2
Distinctive designs such as these shown here should be registered as trade marks.

It may well also be possible and desirable to register distinctive labels and shapes. In the case of labels, it is best to limit the registration to the important elements of the label rather than to all of the details. In many instances, however, those important elements might not be distinctive by themselves. For example, the bowl of rice, the kebab on a skewer and the salt-and-pepper shakers on the Uncle Ben's rice package are probably not separately distinctive. None the less, they have been protected as a composite registration embracing the trade mark and a circular portrait of the man, Uncle Ben, in the way in which they appear on the package. These elements have been considered sufficiently significant in the context of the overall registration to deter infringers in both France and Brazil.

In the case of shapes, many countries permit the registration of shapes as trade marks but such shapes must be

Uncle Ben's Converted är
Sveriges i särklass mest köpta ris.
Och undra på det – den oslagbart
höga kvalitén och den milda, fina
smaken gör Uncle Ben's till
det perfekta valet.
Men har du tänkt på vilka varia-
tionsmöjligheter ris erbjuder, bara
genom lite extra kryddning vid
kokningen. Här ett litet tips från
vårt provkök:

RIS NAPOLETANA.
4 port. Uncle Ben's
Converted Ris
1/3 finhackad gul lök
1 liten hackad vitlöksklyfta
2 msk tomatpuré

Koka riset. Blanda ingredien-
serna till såsen och tillsätt dem
omedelbart före serveringen.

Fläskschnitzel, fläskkotlett eller
stekt fisk.

UncleBens
Alltid perfekt resultat.

Illustration 10.3
The bowl of rice, kebab on skewer and the salt-and-pepper shaker on the Uncle Ben's pack are not separately distinctive yet they have been protected as a composite registration with the trade mark and the portrait of the man, Uncle Ben.

distinctive of the product. That is, they must be used only on the products of a particular manufacturer and they must be recognised by consumers as identifying that product. Good examples of such distinctive shapes are the Coca-Cola waisted soft drink bottle, the Haig whisky 'Pinch' or 'Dimple' bottle, and the triangular shape and packaging of Toblerone chocolates (see also Plate 32).

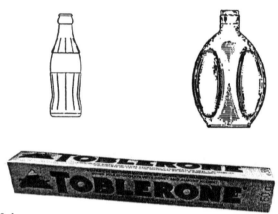

Illustration 10.4
Distinctive product shapes such as these shown here should be registered as trade marks.

Slogans too can be registered as trade marks in many countries. If a slogan, or a similar unique sales proposition (or 'USP'), is a significant part of a power brand's franchise, it should be registered wherever possible. Examples of registered slogan-based trade marks include 'The Taste of Paradise' slogan for Bounty coconut candies, the 'Top Breeders Recommend It' slogan of Pedigree dog foods (Plate 33) and the 'Don't Leave Home Without It' slogan of American Express.

International Aspects

What about protecting a power brand in other languages? What happens when a brand name goes international? Generally it is possible to register the brand name in local languages and it is nearly always highly desirable to do so.

But what should be registered? A translation of the brand name? Yes, provided the brand name has a meaning that can be translated sensibly. For example, Milky Way translates well to Via Lactia in Spanish and to the Japanese equivalent in katakana. But how does one translate made-up names which have no meaning, such as Kodak or Sony? In such cases what is required is not a translation but a transliteration – the *sound* of the trade mark in its base language should be replicated by the sound of the equivalent characters of a quite different language.

In practice, transliterated brand names can provide very powerful trade mark registrations, especially where people hear the brand name as it appears in its base language and say it as best they can in their own languages. In such instances the local language words and/or characters that *sound* closest to the original should be registered. But be careful to ensure that the transliteration does not have a meaning in the local language that is contrary to the image or positioning of the power brand.

Other Distinctive Elements

Other distinctive elements that form a part of a power brand's franchise might also be registrable as trade marks. In the United States, for example, the colour pink has been registered as a trade mark, *per se*, for Fiberglas insulation material, while a particular fragrance has even been registered as a trade mark for sewing thread and embroidery yarn. Sounds too, such as certain spoken words, chiming bells, and specific combinations of musical notes, have been registered as trade marks.

Is it taking things too far to register such things as trade marks? Not in my view – if a trade mark is something that is capable of distinguishing the goods or services of one supplier from those of another (probably the best definition of a trade mark you can get) then clearly they should be registered and protected so as to prevent unauthorised third-party use. So if a sound or a colour or a smell is distinctive of a product from a particular supplier in the same way that a name or a symbol (that is, device, design, logo, and so on) might be, it functions as a trade mark and should be recognised, registered and protected just like a name. The key, of course, is whether a particular element is in fact 'capable of distinguishing' the product, and whether in practice it does so.

In practice, many valuable trade marks, when they start their lives, are not capable of distinguishing one product from another. An example might be the word 'chunky' for dog food, as this could be considered descriptive of any manufacturer's product containing chunks of food. But in the United Kingdom, where Chunky has been used for many years only by one manufacturer, and where both the grocery trade and purchasers of dog food now associate that term only with the products of that manufacturer, Chunky was held to have become distinctive of that manufacturer and hence to be registrable as a trade mark. In effect, the name acquired distinctiveness – it had developed a 'secondary meaning' and thus Chunky became capable of distinguishing products of one manufacturer from those of others.

Unfair Competition

Even, however, where a particular element of a power brand does not quite measure up for registration as a trade mark, or where the trade mark law of a particular country does not allow registration of such elements, protection might nevertheless be provided under a notion of *unfair competition* or by a general statute designed to maintain fair trading or prevent confusion among the public. Such forms of protection are all based on the notion that one person should not take commercial advantage of the reputation and goodwill of another person.

Although the standards for this sort of protection vary from country to country and often depend upon the facts of each particular case, it is generally the case that an infringement of one's intellectual property rights can be stopped if there is actual confusion, or sometimes a likelihood of confusion, or even where there is a sense that an inherently unfair or improper activity is involved. Protection of this kind can be very powerful. It is often available in addition to the remedies provided under trade mark law. Indeed, in some instances it may be the *only* protection available, particularly where for some reason trade mark law is not applicable.

A noteworthy example of this occurred recently in Germany and involved a small company well known for dealing in novelty items incorporating popular trade marks, including salacious corruptions of such trade marks. The company had indeed already successfully defended itself against attacks for distributing posters based on Lusthansa (*sic*) and a very rude expression for which the automobile trade mark BMW was an acronym. They were stopped by the courts, however, from continuing to sell condoms in small packets dressed with the classic Mars confectionery logo and carrying a sexually explicit corruption of the slogan 'A Mars a day helps you work, rest and play.' Even though trade mark protection was not available because the products were so very different, the trial court was offended by the derogation of the famous candy product, the great reputation of which was obviously being traded upon. An important additional factor was that children might mistakenly buy the condom packet thinking it was a candy bar! As a result the lower court's injunction was upheld on appeal.

Trade Mark Corruption

It is said that imitation is the sincerest form of flattery, but who wants to be flattered when the imitation in question is the use of a valuable marketing property in a totally unsuitable context? Examples of such corruption include a modified Coca-Cola logo on a T-shirt purporting to exhort the use of cocaine, a leading candy product strategically placed as the only covering for a young woman featured in the centrefold of *Playboy* magazine, the salacious corruption of a famous slogan to form the punch line of a greeting card, the use of another famous slogan in the lyrics in a lewd rap song, and a depiction in a pornographic newspaper of the wholesome Pillsbury 'Doughboy' in a sexual act.

What should one do about such things? Clearly, acting to stop this kind of abuse of a power brand is very likely to generate a great deal of publicity but this may only call attention to the unpleasantness. Indeed, it could even play into the hands of the unscrupulous characters who do these things, enabling them to sell more T-shirts, magazines or music. And, after taking action, what if the courts refuse to stop the activity? For example, in the USA and in some other countries certain uses might be considered 'artistic expressions' that are protected as 'free speech', or merely as 'parodies' that no one would take seriously as originating from or sponsored by the true proprietor of the power brand. In such circumstances it is sometimes better to do nothing, to let the matter pass quietly into history. But doing nothing takes courage; it might also give confidence to others and embolden them to continue such activities.

All things considered, unless there is a strong reason in particular to the contrary, swift and aggressive action is the best policy in matters of this kind. Even if such action proves unsuccessful, there is no harm in having a reputation for vigorously protecting your power brands. In fact, it is probably highly desirable to be known as a tiger who will go after anyone who tampers with your marketing properties. Knowing that trade mark abuse is likely to be attacked quickly and aggressively will make would-be offenders think twice before trying anything on.

Other Initiatives

A number of further steps can be taken to improve one's ability to protect a brand name and to enlarge the brand's breadth of protection. Registering the trade mark in as many classes as possible is one way, but that can be expensive,[2] especially if it must be done in a large number of countries. None the less, many companies register their power brands in all or virtually all classes, at least in their countries of primary interest. They are then confronted, however, by the requirement of most countries to *use* a mark in order to retain valid registrations. That means, in the case of Sony Corporation, that they would have to sell Sony brand chewing gum to keep their Class 29 registration, lubricating oil to stay valid in Class 4 and they would have to operate a trucking company to retain a service mark in Class 39! Moreover, in many countries, now including the USA, such sales would have to be of a commercially significant volume to count; token sales of five or so cases of Sony lubricating oil every few years would not impress the courts.

But is it appropriate that Sony Corporation has to be active in the oil, food, and transportation businesses merely to maintain its trade mark registrations? I do not think so. Consider too that many countries require that, at the time of applying to register a trade mark, the applicant has a genuine intent to use that trade mark in a commercial manner. Could Sony pass that test with respect to, say, automobiles? Again, it is doubtful. Overall, the practice of registering one's trade marks across the world in unrelated classes is extremely expensive and, in many cases, of doubtful value. It benefits the incomes of trade mark attorneys around the world and the fees paid to foreign governments for dubious trade mark registrations are also, no doubt, a welcome source of foreign exchange but, for the trade mark owner, the benefits are more limited. In some cases, however, this strategy needs to be considered.

Then there is the problem of how many trade marks need to be registered. If there really is only one power brand within the company, as perhaps in the case of Sony, then there may be little or no problem. But what about branded goods companies such as Procter & Gamble, Unilever or Nestlé that are blessed with dozens, even hundreds of power brands? They have all the problems I have already detailed but on a much larger scale.

As a practical matter, therefore, a power brand should be registered in the classes covering the goods and/or services for which it is used and, if possible, in those classes covering related goods and services. For example, if one wished to protect a confectionery trade mark the 'core' class would be Class 30 (coffees, breads, pastries, confectionery, etc.) but it would probably also be prudent to register the trade mark in Class 29 (other foodstuffs, including meats, etc.), Class 31 (fresh fruit and vegetables, etc.), Class 32 (soft drinks, beers, etc.) and even Class 5 (medicines and dietetic products, but including medicated confectionery such as throat lozenges). Clearly, careful thought must be given to ensure that the registrations of a power brand cover all appropriate trade mark classes.

International Arrangements

There are several international arrangements that serve to facilitate the registration and protection of trade marks. The largest, oldest and most important of these is the Paris Convention for the Protection of Industrial Property, which came into being in 1883 and which has been revised several times since. About 100 countries belong to it. Important features of the Paris Convention include the fact that foreigners benefit from the same rights as nationals of each member country; that foreigners who apply to register a new trade mark in member countries within six months of filing in their home country are given 'priority' over others filing within that period; and that well-known or famous trade marks (such as 'power brands') are given an especially broad range of protection.

The Madrid Agreement (or 'Arrangement' or 'Union') of 1891, another important international treaty, provides a system whereby the World Intellectual Property Organisation, an agency of the United Nations based in Geneva, Switzerland, can be used to file an application to obtain a so-called 'International Registration' that can be extended to as many of the twenty-nine signatory countries as an applicant might wish. A new Protocol for the Madrid Arrangement, which will come into being and provide additional features, is expected to attract many new countries, including the USA and the UK.

In addition, within the European Union a Regulation to create a single trade mark law is expected to come into force in the mid-1990s; thus a single application could lead to a Trade Mark Registration that is effective throughout all of the Member States of the EU. Other regional arrangements, both extant and proposed, can also be of value for the registration and protection of power brands.

Importance of Use

After a trade mark is registered, most countries require that it be used in order for the registration to remain valid. This requirement exists to provide a basis for removing unused trade marks from the register, thus making them available to others who might wish to adopt and use them.[3] But when must the use begin? Before registration? At registration? After registration? With few if any significant exceptions, all countries allow a period of several years following registration before the trade mark owner must begin to make use of the mark for some or all of the goods for which it is registered[4]. Five years is the most usual period, but after that the registration becomes vulnerable to an attack for its cancellation from the register.

The period following registration during which use of a trade mark is not required is very important. It might seem, at first sight, that the trade mark owner has gained an unfair advantage over others – the owner has in effect 'annexed' the mark so that others cannot use it, but is not obliged to use it himself. In fact, the reason for this apparent leniency on the part of legislators is to give the owner a reasonable opportunity to make the investment necessary to launch the branded product or service. No one would commit to packaging, advertising, production and distribution of a new branded product or service if trade mark rights to the brand name were not secured by registration.

Line Extensions

In recent years there has been a marked trend on the part of power brand owners towards the extension of the range of goods or services marketed under their brands. Generally this is done for sound marketing reasons but such line extensions – that is, the introduction of products substantially different from those of the parent or original brand but under the same brand name – also serve to increase both the problems, but also eventually the scope, of trade mark protection. Thus what was once known as a brand name only for a certain product or type of product can, though line extension, become known for other products. An example is the Mars brand, which has been known worldwide for many years as a chocolate-covered nougat and caramel candy bar (Plate 34). Now, Mars is also the brand name of a block chocolate bar, a milk drink, and an ice cream bar (Plate 37). The result of a line extension programme is that the brand name becomes associated with a wider variety of products and this in turn entitles the brand name to a broader scope of protection (see Plates 35 and 36 for other examples of the Mars portfolio).

Illustration 10.5
The Mars brand has been successfully extended to ice-cream bars and milk drinks.

A further benefit of line extensions is that they help greatly in preventing a trade mark, especially a power brand, from becoming generic. Many power brands tend to become synonymous with their products, that is, they come to be thought of as the descriptive name of the product, a tendency which is a death trap for the brand name because when a trade mark becomes generic it is no longer protectable – it becomes available for use by everyone as the common name of a product. What an irony! Every marketing person would like nothing better than to have his brand name become the everyday term for its product. But if that happens, the brand name no longer distinguishes his product from the same products of others so it will have come to mean *all and any* such products and is consequently lost. Examples of US trademarks that became generic and were lost include aspirin, cellophane, escalator, yo-yo and nylon.

Very many power brands are at risk of becoming generic including Xerox photocopiers, Kodak cameras and films, Kleenex facial tissues, Hoover vacuum cleaners, Frigidaire refrigerators, Formica laminates, Jacuzzi bathtubs and Coke cola drinks. The renown of these brand names causes many people to use them generically when referring to all such products, a usage which puts the brands at risk. Owners of these valuable marks are, however, acutely aware of the problem and guard their marks particularly carefully for this reason.

But what is it about line extensions that help to keep a brand name from becoming generic? The answer is that the use of the name for more than one type of product ensures that the brand no longer means only one product. Thus if the brand name is used for several different products, it cannot become the common descriptive name for any of them. Vaseline is a case in point and a good example of how line extensions have helped to move a power brand away from becoming generic. For decades Vaseline was the trade mark only for a leading refined petroleum jelly product with which it was virtually synonymous. Now, however, Vaseline is also used for moisturising lotion, hand and nail lotion, facial soap, and for lip balm. The brand name no longer means only petroleum jelly so the danger of genericisation has receded.

Lysol is another example. It signified for years a strong, alkali-based cleaning composition but, with line extensions, Lysol products now include liquid, solid and spray air fresheners, laundry detergents and bleach. So as well as it making good marketing and commercial sense to capitalise on the reputation of a popular power brand it can also be a key preventive measure in stopping a brand from becoming generic.

Finally, while we are still on the subject of line extensions, I would like to return once again to the important issue of trade mark registrations. Frequently companies only register their brand names, even their power brands, for the narrow range of goods or services on which the brand name first appeared. Not infrequently, when a company decides to extend its brand, closer examination reveals that the brand owner does not have any registered rights to the brand name in the proposed new area. There have even been instances where companies, in perhaps a fit of over-generosity, have given away their rights in a related area to a third party and have subsequently found themselves barred from undertaking an apparently entirely legitimate brand extension. So if you are planning any line extensions, check your trade mark registrations as a matter of urgency and if you have any deficiency in this area fix it immediately!

Licensing

Another way to enhance trade mark protection of a power brand – and, importantly, to extend protection to products other than those currently sold under the brand name – is to license the use of the brand name on a range of premium and promotional products. Such an approach allows the power brand to be used in a powerful way on a diversity of products, but without the brand owner having to get involved in the manufacture of such products.

These so-called 'collateral' products can be used to support the advertising and promotion of products sold under the power brand name, can act as an additional source of income and can help to extend the brand's legal franchise. Using a power brand name on such collateral products provides a legitimate basis for registration of the brand name as a trade mark in the trade mark classes within which such collateral products fall.

Examples abound of this kind of protective activity; who has not seen a Heineken beach towel, a Coca-Cola ice chest, a Marlboro coffee mug, an umbrella emblazoned with the McDonald's Golden Arch logo, or a cap with Monsieur

Bibendum, the Michelin tyre man logo? Such applications can have great advertising and promotional value, they can be a useful (but seldom huge) source of licensing income and they help to extend protection for the respective power brands far beyond beer, cola, cigarettes, hamburgers or tyres. Of course, not all power brands are suitable for collateral products, but the owner of a power brand should at least consider whether it is possible to expand the scope of protection for his power brand in such a way.

Proper Usage

Any programme to guard against a power brand becoming generic must include proper usage of the trade mark by the owner[5], education of others about usage of the brand name and active 'policing' of misuses of the trade mark. Simple rules for proper usage of a trade mark include using the mark as it is registered; not using either a plural or a singular or a possessive form of the mark unless that is the way it is registered; using the trade mark properly as an adjective rather than as a noun (for example, always speak of a Kleenex *tissue*, never a Kleenex); always therefore using a generic or dictionary word in association with the trade mark (a good practice even in countries where, strictly speaking, it is not necessary); visually distinguishing the mark by a different colour or type style or by quotation marks or by underlining; and indicating that the trade mark is in fact a trade mark either through the ® symbol, the ™ symbol or the ℠ symbol.[6] (Use of such symbols is good practice even in countries where such use is not strictly required by law.)

In addition, brand owners should also educate others about the rules of proper usage, especially in relation to power brands. Many will be familiar with the advertising campaign of Kimberly-Clark Corporation, Xerox Corporation and American Express about proper usage of their extremely valuable power brands, Kleenex facial tissues, Xerox copier products and, in the case of American Express, slogans such as 'Don't leave home without it'.

The policing of trade marks can take many forms. One way is to ensure, through the use of a team of inspectors, that whenever someone asks for a Pepsi Cola or a Coca-Cola soft drink they in fact get what they ask for and do not receive a competitor's soft drink. Another is to correct wrong usage of trade marks in dictionaries, newspapers and magazines, in films and on television. The prevention of counterfeiting, perhaps the ultimate form of trade mark infringement and misuse, is also essential to the preservation of any power brand.

Harmonisation

Another way in which power brands can be protected is through proper 'harmonisation' of the brand name, the packaging design, and of advertising and promotional materials. Such harmonisation can be extremely helpful from a marketing point of view and it can also help to strengthen trade mark protection. This is because the legal protection afforded to power brands depends in large part on recognition, not only of the brand name itself, but also of the logo, the label design and the packaging. It is sensible therefore to harmonise these elements, that is to use them in the same way on different varieties and products so as to achieve the greatest impact. Conversely, if one allows substantial differences and variations in the way in which these elements are applied then confusion may be caused as well as a consequent dilution of the impact of the power brand.

Harmonisation need not however mean everything being identical. It means the systematic and consistent application of designs, features and graphics, though perhaps the most important of these is the standardisation of the graphic form of the brand name. Examples of a standardised approach through stylised lettering include Dunhill, Kellogg's and Harrods. Ford and IBM are good examples of standardised use of stylised logos. Moreover, the brand name should also be presented always in the same colour so that the commonality of approach and repetition of key elements

Illustration 10.6
The famous trade marks shown here are good examples of power brands that are applied appropriately and consistently wherever they appear.

and colours enables people interested in the products to associate them readily with a common origin. Logos such as the blue and white BMW roundel, the red and white checkerboard squares of Ralston Purina and the tan, red and dark blue plaid design of Burberry are especially powerful symbols in this regard.

The same colours or colour combinations of labels or packages can also be used to create associations between the different varieties and products offered under a power brand. Food products under the Uncle Ben's brand, for example, always have the brand name in its distinctive letterstyle and blue colouring against a particular shade of orange across the top quarter or so of the front of the package. Other graphics on the remainder of the front of the package vary according to the different varieties and types of products such as rice, flavoured rice dishes, sauces, pastas and other foods. In this way, purchasers can identify and select the different products and varieties covered by the power brand but, at the same time, harmonisation of the elements of the brand presentation serves to bring together the entire range of products under the one brand image. Moreover, this reinforcement of the brand's core values greatly enhances recognition of the power brand and thus helps to broaden the scope of its protection.

Final Thoughts

In summary, protection of a power brand must not be left to chance. Power brands are valuable assets and it is well worth making a substantial investment in terms of time, effort and money to protect and preserve them. A thoughtful and thorough analysis of all the elements that go to make up the core values of the brand should also be carried out at regular intervals and should involve both the marketing and the legal people responsible for the brand – marketing personnel can detail those elements of the brand which are considered to be fundamental to brand success, while legal personnel can identify how best to protect these. Such cooperation will give a power brand what it deserves – the best chance for a long and happy life.

Notes

1. Whenever I mention product trade marks in this chapter the same remarks will normally apply to service marks.
2. There are thirty-four classes for products, and eight classes for services, in the International Classification System for Trade Marks and Service Marks.
3. Remember, however, that continuous use of a trade mark enables its registration to be maintained and repeatedly renewed, providing what amounts to perpetual rights.
4. In the United States, use of a trade mark *is* required before it can be registered. There is, however, a period of as much as three years following acceptance of an application for registration in which to begin use.
5. Many companies have manuals and pamphlets about proper usage of their trade marks and some even have

videos and internal training programmes. Some of these are available upon request from the companies concerned. The US Trademark Association also has several publications on proper trade mark usage.

6. Though the ® and ™ symbols are often used interchange-ably, the former should only be used where registered rights actually exist while the latter symbol can be used to indicate proprietary rights whether registered or otherwise. The ℠ symbol should be used only on service marks.

BRAND-BASED STRATEGY AND STRUCTURE: THE SCANDINAVIAN EXPERIENCE

11

Carsten Dahlman
Senior Partner
SIAR BOSSARD

Introduction

For decades the Scandinavian market has not taken much notice of branding. But a number of recent events have combined to change this indifference, with the result that branding has now become of central importance to many Scandinavian businesses.

This chapter explains how this 'revolution' has come about and, in particular, how those organisations that have developed real 'brand-based' cultures are far more likely to succeed in branded goods markets than those that have not. Although most of the content of this chapter is drawn from my experience of the Scandinavian market, many of the concepts and principles set out here hold equally well, I believe, for any country where brand power has not yet become readily apparent.

Trends in Scandinavia – Overall

Multinational branded goods companies have begun in recent years to expand their sphere of influence to include Scandinavia. Foreign brands, well supported and commanding strong consumer appeal, are becoming more and more commonplace. Scandinavian companies have been forced to respond to this challenge with their own brand-based marketing strategies. This trend is particularly evident in the industry which I have selected to be the focal point of discussion for this chapter – the food industry.

But although the competitive threat from foreign branded goods companies has been the main driving force behind the change in attitude in Scandinavia towards brands and branding, there have been a number of other contributory factors.

Development of own label brands

Historically, own label market share in the Scandinavian market has been less than 5 per cent compared to 30 per cent or 40 per cent in the rest of Europe. One reason for this disparity has been the strong wholesale orientation of many Scandinavian retailers. Increased competition and a more sophisticated marketing approach has led many Scandinavian retail chains to become aware of the potential for well managed and well designed own label brands. Scandinavian food manufacturers will have to improve their own brand offer if they are to remain competitive.

Recognition of the importance of 'pull' rather than 'push'

For decades the main focus in the Scandinavian food industry has been on sales and distribution in the domestic market. Scandinavian food manufacturers have therefore followed a 'push' strategy in their confrontation with national and international competitors, unlike their European counterparts whose increasing focus is on matching consumer demand with targeted products, thereby creating much more of a 'pull' phenomenon. The resource allocated to brand development in Scandinavian companies to create this 'pull' phenomenon has so far been minimal. But this too is changing.

Deregulation

Bulk food suppliers (such as dairy producers, meat producers, sugar companies and so on) have benefited from the protective measures introduced by a series of Scandinavian governments. Barriers to free trade include high agricultural subsidies granted to local farmers and punitive tariffs on imports. In many other European countries protective measures brought about by government intervention have been broken down – the example of the French dairy industry being a case in point. Of all the Scandinavian countries, only Denmark comes anywhere near the European norm. But a new wave of deregulation is sweeping through Scandinavia as it prepares to join the European Community and it is highly likely that the restrictions on free trade endemic in many of Scandinavia's food markets will change radically over the next few years. This will allow foreign brands to play a far more significant rôle in the Scandinavian market than hitherto.

The Scandinavian Market Place

There are a number of important changes taking place in the Scandinavian market, some caused by external factors and some by internal factors.

External factors

Changes taking place outside the Scandinavian market but which are making an impact within Scandinavia include the following:

Figure 11.1 Factors creating change in the Scandinavian consumer market

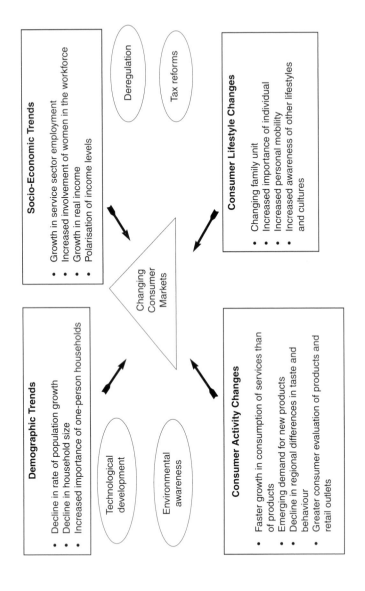

The European Community

The advent of the Single European Market has encouraged increased trade between Member States of the Community. Companies are becoming more used to trading outside their immediate borders. The inevitable consequence of this for Scandinavia is that more foreign competitors will come and are coming into the market.

The media

Developments in the media, such as the increasing influence of satellite TV with genuine Europe-wide coverage and increasing competition leading to reduced costs for advertising space, mean that large multinationals have become far more sophisticated in their purchasing of advertising. Rates are better and the commissions paid to agencies are keener than ever before. With the advent of commercial television in the Swedish market only quite recently, it is clear that foreign manufacturers with their long experience in the use of this medium will be able to make aggressive and effective inroads into the market.

'One market' status

Multinationals look at Scandinavia as one homogeneous market and organise their production and distribution systems accordingly. Large economies of scale result.

The international retailers

The big international retailers are looking very carefully at the Scandinavian market. If they decide to invest in Scandinavia, the existing complacency in the domestic retail trade will by necessity need to be translated into a much more aggressive marketing-oriented approach. One inevitable consequence of this would be the development of own label brands by domestic retailers. For decades Scandinavian food manufacturers have not had to concern themselves with this threat.

These external factors will convert what is currently only a mildly competitive market into a much more aggressive environment where national and international suppliers and retailers will be fighting hard for supremacy.

Internal factors

Internal factors which have frustrated the development and appreciation of branding techniques in Scandinavia include the following:

Lack of brand management skill

Brand development in most Scandinavian food companies is left to young product managers working in small marketing departments who are heavily reliant on their advertising agencies for strategic advice. Advertising agencies clearly have an important rôle to play in terms of developing the most effective way in which to communicate an agreed brand strategy to the market but for the advertising agency to be involved in actually developing that strategy seems to be devolving too much responsibility to an outsider.

Brand management not given sufficient organisational status

The status of brand management within organisations is inferior to that of operational or functional management. This means that important strategic decisions regarding the future development of a company's brand portfolio do not receive the attention they deserve.

Sales skills versus branding skills

Strong sales and distribution resource has in the past compensated for weak brands. Only rarely has the power of the brand been stronger than the distribution power of the organisation. In the new market environment sales and distribution power will be of subsidiary importance to the need to develop power brands.

Short-term tactics versus long-term strategic development

The adoption of short-term tactics, such as price-driven sales promotion initiatives, together with the absence of any genuine power brands within the market has led many companies to ignore branding altogether.

✳   ✳   ✳

It is clear from the foregoing that Scandinavian companies are not well equipped to fight any kind of brand war. Significant changes in attitude and corporate culture need to take place before Scandinavian companies can hope to become competitive.

But of course not all companies have to become wholly brand-oriented. A company that manufactures a commodity which has no functional point of difference, like sugar, has no need for branding. Consumers will buy such products on price and availability and not on brand image. Such companies will become dedicated production-oriented suppliers. On the other hand, companies manufacturing products which have far greater functional points of difference (for example, confectionery products) have a clear need to develop a brand-oriented approach. Certain companies will need to adopt a brand-oriented approach for some of their businesses and a production-oriented approach for others. A Finnish bakery, for example, may have a range of branded cookies in one division but be producing generic bulk bread in another. Whilst there is a clear need for stronger brand management, this must always be seen in the context of the realities of the business in question and its competitive environment.

What is the Most Effective Organisational Structure for a Brand-Based Company?

Very little seems to have been written about the kind of organisational structure that is most likely to encourage effective brand management and, as mentioned earlier, many

Scandinavian companies have tended to ignore branding altogether, partly because they tend to be more production-oriented but also because the structure of the marketplace, the lack of real retail power and the strong protectionist influence of the government have meant that branding has not had much influence.

Those Scandinavian companies that have managed to develop a power brand have been content to rely on that one brand without bothering to follow up with a second or third brand in order to build a proper brand portfolio. Take some Swedish examples: Vin & Spritecentralen established the Absolut vodka brand on an international scale, but has not launched a second comparably powerful brand. Pågen AB is the most successful bakery in Scandinavia and has had considerable success in the European market with its Krisprolls brand but, again, a second brand has not yet been launched. The largest Scandinavian confectionery company Freija-Marabou has been very successful in establishing the Daim brand outside Scandinavia but, to date, has not been able to replicate this success with another.

When these brand owners were asked to explain what had been the most influential factors behind the success of these brands, the most common replies were: 'We were lucky'; 'It was a brilliant idea that could not be repeated'; 'Our timing was right'; and so on. In other words, the success stories were more a result of chance and coincidence than the product of a well thought-out brand strategy.

But brand strategies can only be developed in those companies whose organisational structure allows such strategies to be encouraged. I firmly believe that a company's organisational structure can be instrumental in determining whether or not it is to be successful in the branded goods area. Some company cultures are more suited than others in providing the right environment for healthy brand development. Some companies have control systems which are designed to monitor and enhance the performance of strong brands, while other companies have no systems of control whatsoever, leading to a total lack of knowledge about their brands' performance.

My own view is that a company's success or failure in launching and developing brands depends entirely on that company's organisational structure, culture, systems, resources and management philosophy.

The Essential Conditions for Powerful Brand-Based Companies

The nature of a company's culture, structure, systems and resource base depends largely on the dynamics of the particular industry in which it competes. Companies competing in the mining or forestry business focus their efforts on the location and extraction of raw materials. Companies competing in the technological field or in pharmaceuticals know that success lies in investing heavily in research and development in order to produce innovative products that meet a need in the market. Companies competing in the consulting services business know that their most important assets are their people and that the key to success is providing a better service than anyone else. The optimum culture, structure, systems and resource base of a *brand-based* company are all dependent on the particular characteristics of the industry in which the company competes and on the recognition that its most important assets are its brands.

Brand-based culture

At every level of a successful brand-based company – especially at top management level – people share the belief that brands are the company's most important assets. They endeavour to safeguard and protect these assets for the long-term and they seek continuity and consistency in brand management. The brand-based company culture is also characterised by strong commitment on the part of top management to the development of the company's leading brands. The whole organisation, not merely the marketing department, gives support and priority to its brands.

An orientation towards meeting the needs and requirements of consumers does not merely start in the marketing
department, but is emphasised and understood at the highest
levels in the organisation. It is common practice within such
organisations for corporate strategy development to be
informed in large part by brand strategy.

Brand-based organisational structure

In a brand-based organisation, key decisions concerning
brands are made by top management. The structure itself is
brand-oriented, with line management serving brand management and not the other way round. Brand management is
given the authority and responsibility to manage brands as
'companies within the company'. Full co-operation exists
between the marketing department, responsible for creating
and sustaining the brand's image and well-being thereby
stimulating and maintaining demand for the brand, and the
sales department, responsible for ensuring that the brand
achieves the widest possible distribution.

Brand-based systems

In a brand-based organisation, all strategic planning must be
based upon a profound understanding of that organisation's
brands. Short-term decisions must be taken within the context
of an appreciation of the organisation's long-term brand-
building goals. The systems that provide top management
with the information necessary to make decisions are also
brand-based. Such systems must be designed so as to enable
top management to assess true brand profitability and to
monitor the effectiveness of brand managers in reaching their
targets. A means must be established for measuring the
acceptability or otherwise of a brand's performance in
relation to the investment in advertising and support that is
put behind it. Management should be able to calculate the

genuine profitability of every brand within a company's portfolio.

Brand-based management resources

The brand management rôle should be given the respect and appreciation it deserves. Brand managers, with their extensive areas of responsibility, must be supported by co-operative line managers. The traditional tug-of-war between marketing and sales or between marketing and finance must be replaced by creative co-operation with all parties focused on developing the brands. Top management must supplement their understanding of the national market with a much stronger understanding of the international marketplace so that threats from foreign companies making inroads into the domestic market can be identified earlier, as can opportunities for international expansion.

How to Become a Brand-Based Company

It is not easy to become a brand-based company. A company whose culture has been steeped in the production and distribution of goods to wholesalers will not be able to change into a brand-based consumer-oriented company overnight. It takes time and effort to make such a change. Most important of all it takes a complete change of corporate attitude and personality.

Experienced gained from our work in this field has persuaded us that it can be very helpful to divide businesses into four main groups or 'business structures', as follows:

(i)   Production-oriented

(ii) Sales-oriented

(iii) Marketing-oriented

(iv) Brand-oriented and retail-oriented

I shall describe each of these in turn.

(i) Production-oriented companies

Production-oriented food companies in Scandinavia are slowly becoming more sales-oriented and, as part of an overall rationalisation of their unwieldy product ranges, are examining the practicalities and appropriateness of alternative branding structures. Some are adopting a branded system (where each product is branded separately) and others are adopting a monolithic system (where the corporate brand is used as the only brand for all products). This phenomenon is discussed more fully later in this chapter.

An important task for management in production-oriented firms is to develop a more aggressive sales organisation and to take the first steps towards developing brand-based strategies and a corresponding brand management structure (see Figure 11.2). This could be described as taking a step to the right from a 'zero-situation' to a 'push' situation.

Producer co-operatives in the food industry, in markets that have until now benefited from a protectionist environment, currently face a major challenge requiring proactive corporate management. A change of emphasis must take place away from production-oriented business systems to a more sales and marketing and/or brand-oriented approach. This will necessitate a form of cultural revolution to enable significant shifts in power from production to sales and marketing. It will also necessitate the identification of external resources in the form of new international joint venture partners and new management, all of which is required to ensure that cultural change actually takes place.

(ii) Sales-oriented companies

The main difference between sales-oriented and marketing-oriented firms is that a strong retail perspective exists in the former and a strong end-consumer orientation in the latter. The task for management in sales-oriented firms is to take a further step to the right and to combine established strengths in sales and distribution with a more targeted marketing

Figure 11.2 Different types of business structure

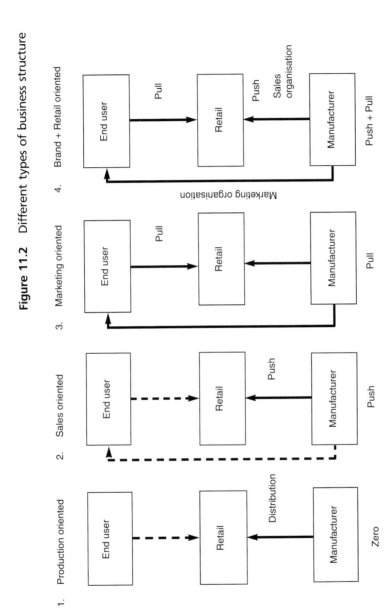

approach. The task is to find out what consumers want to buy and then to match this need with attractive, well branded products in order to develop a 'pull' phenomenon.

In sales-oriented corporations, the rôle of corporate management must be to encourage line management to develop a more pronounced marketing-oriented structure, to ensure that they exploit their brands fully and to create strong consumer loyalty. Corporate management must ensure that operating business unit management develops retail strategies which complement their brand strategies and back-up support systems.

(iii) Marketing-oriented companies

Many international branded goods companies fit in the marketing-oriented category. Marketing-oriented firms exploit their brands through skilful image building and communication strategies, but fail to realise the full potential of their brands through revitalisation, extension, transferal or 'internationalisation' programmes. Marketing-oriented firms must aim to build a powerful brand image for the end-consumer and need to focus efforts in two areas; first, they need to become more skilful at 'brand engineering' and, secondly, they need to put in place more sophisticated retail strategies, thereby combining the 'push' and 'pull' dynamics as effectively and profitably as possible.

In 'overfocused' marketing-oriented firms, where too much emphasis tends to be put on short-term promotions to the end-consumer and not enough on building either brand equities or long-term relationships with the retail trade, the rôle of corporate management is to balance the powerful 'pull' orientation with a stronger 'push' orientation. Long-term resource for brand engineering must thus be provided and corporate management must also make sure that an overall retail strategy is developed. Corporate management must in addition involve itself in developing an international organisation which ensures consistency of brand identity and brand image internationally.

(iv) Brand-oriented and retail-oriented companies

The company whose culture, structure, systems and resources are geared towards the development and enhancement of brands is the true winner in today's competitive markets. The company which is both brand and retail-oriented has the ability to exploit brand power to develop a powerful and profitable business. Exploiting brand power requires not only an understanding of how to develop a power brand but also how to make it flourish in the retail trade. Companies like Guinness, Grand Metropolitan and BSN have all developed cultures, structures, systems and resources which enable them to compete highly effectively on an international scale.

The Rôle of Management

I have already stressed that the only way to become a genuine brand-based company is to make top management take ultimate responsibility for brands and the development of brand strategy. The rôle of management is to provide the structure, culture, systems and resources that will enable the company to develop and maintain a portfolio of genuine power brands.

With this in mind I believe that there are a number of general brand-based tasks which should always be the responsibility of corporate management (see Figure 11.3). In particular, corporate management must:

(i) Establish a culture and structure that will allow a brand-oriented approach to business strategy to flourish.

(ii) Make sure that internal resources are used effectively in improving production efficiencies, in developing new products, in supporting sales and marketing initiatives and in enhancing quality control.

(iii) Encourage each operating unit to develop long-term business plans with brands forming a key element of such plans.

Figure 11.3 The characteristics of different business structures

1. Production Oriented	2. Sales Oriented	3. Marketing Oriented	4. Brand + Retail Oriented
Key characteristics	**Key characteristics**	**Key characteristics**	**Key characteristics**
- Raw material orientation - Production focused - National perspective - Logistics - Non-brand orientation - Corporate name = product names common practice - Small or non-existent marketing organisation	- Sales and distribution focused - Retail oriented - Low degree of consumer orientation - Small marketing organisation - Product range ambitions - House brand orientation common practice - Unexploited brands - Push strategy	- Marketing and communication oriented - Monobrands and housebrands - Strong consumer orientation - Image building focused - International - Strong marketing organisation - Pull strategy	- Strong ability to develop the overall strategy based on the brands - Strong brand based culture and organisation - "Brand engineering" competence - Strong monobrands - The brands fully exploited and nurtured in a long-term perspective - Developed retail strategies - Strong sales organisation - Pull + push
Examples	**Examples**	**Examples**	**Examples**
Scandinavian: - Bulk food suppliers (e.g. meat, cheese, sugar) European: - Business-to-business firms (e.g. building material, paper, steel)	Scandinavian: - A majority of the food suppliers (e.g. bakeries, breweries, confectionery) European: - Small and medium-sized national food suppliers	Scandinavian: - Usually the subsidiaries of international firms (e.g. Procter & Gamble) and a small (but growing) number of more advanced Scandinavians	Scandinavian: - Advanced brand-based firms with strong pull + push organisation (e.g. Carlsberg) European: - Nestlé, Unilever etc.

(iv) Encourage operating management to exploit strong brands fully in terms of revitalisation, extension, internationalisation, and so on.

(v) Provide a means of evaluating brand assets, particularly in the case of acquisitions, and implement a system to ensure that brand assets are neither under-valued nor over-valued.

(vi) Ensure that acquired brands are not damaged or destroyed post-acquisition; it is far too often the case that after an acquisition some of the acquired assets are destroyed simply because integration of the two organisations is carried out in an insensitive manner.

(vii) Establish a brand-oriented culture and management philosophy and make sure the internal organisational structure reflects the realities of the external environment.

(viii) Finally, insist upon an organisational structure and brand-based control system which will facilitate cultural change and give the brand assets the space and environment in which to be developed effectively.

Brand-Based Company Structures

In conclusion, it might be helpful to dwell for a few moments on the various kinds of structure employed by brand-based companies.

The monolithic structure

A monolithic brand structure is adopted by those companies who use one brand for all their products and services. Examples of companies which adopt a monolithic structure include IBM, Mercedes, Volvo, Porsche and Sony.

The advantages of this approach are that the company can pursue a very strong and single-minded brand strategy. The brand management task is the responsibility of everyone within the organisation from the board to the lowest paid employee. Marketing becomes highly cost effective since there is only one brand to promote. The success of one part of the group can be shared by another part of the group since all share the same brand name. The problem of course is that the bad news encountered by one part of the group will be shared by the rest of the group. When the Exxon Valdez ran aground off the coast of Alaska consumers boycotted petrol stations right across the USA because of the ensuing controversy over damage to the environment. If the ship had not been branded with the Exxon name, then the company might have been able to avoid a great deal of the damaging public relations from the incident.

One obvious rôle for management within such organisations is to ensure that even the most detailed decisions concerning brand management are taken at the top level. This means that corporate managers become, in reality, brand managers. A typical problem encountered in these companies is brand over-extension (where the corporate brand becomes so over-extended that its impact is diluted). To counteract this requires a 'Back to the core identity' type of corporate initiative.

The monolithic brand can be used in combination with individual product brands in areas where the corporate brand does not have the right identity and image. This approach is a move towards the 'house brand' or 'endorsed' structure.

The house brand or endorsed structure

A house brand or endorsed structure is one where the corporate name stands for a guarantee of quality or as an endorsing device to lend strength and support to underlying product brands. General Motors, Nestlé, Ford and Marabou provide examples of this sort of organisation.

The house brand or endorsed structure aims to combine the benefits of the monolithic structure with the need to develop separate targeted brands for products which have their own distinctive personalities. Moreover, the risk of the corporate brand becoming damaged because of problems encountered elsewhere in the group can be reduced by limiting the exposure given to the corporate brand and maximising the exposure given to the product brand. One potential disadvantage is that a house brand can be used to endorse so many different products that it loses its crispness and identity. Over-extension is a common development trap in companies which pursue an endorsement philosophy.

The rôle of corporate management within such an organisation is to formulate clear brand management rules and guidelines and to ensure that these are followed strictly.

The product brand structure

Corporations which follow the product brand or multibrand model include companies like Unilever and Procter & Gamble. In such a structure, the name of the corporation is kept quite distinct from the names of the underlying product brands. This is particularly common in international companies who are very skilled at brand building in industries where there is enough sales volume to allow individual brands to flourish as large-scale international businesses (for example, food, beverages, detergents).

The advantage of this approach is that the brand can be positioned in a clear and focused fashion to consumers in terms of image, quality, price and values; consumer loyalty to the brand can thus be improved. This is, however, an expensive structure and requires significant resource and input from all levels of the corporation.

Corporate management pursuing this structure must have a proven brand-based culture and organisation. In comparison to companies which follow the monolithic approach, multibrand-oriented companies must rely to a higher extent on individual operating unit, marketing and product management and must provide support to the operating units through well developed brand-oriented control systems. One problem area is how to handle the inevitable cannibalism that will take place between competing brands in the same portfolio. A common solution to this is to establish 'category' or product group responsibility so that diseconomies on a group basis can be minimised.

Conclusion

A final word. Those companies who recognise that brands are their most important assets must accept at the highest levels of management that long-term corporate strategy development must be brand-oriented if the company is to succeed. For many companies this will involve making radical changes to corporate strategy. This is the lesson which many Scandinavian companies are learning right now.

ASSESSING BRAND VALUE **12**

Michael Birkin
Group Chief Executive
INTERBRAND GROUP PLC

Introduction

The value of a brand, like that of any other similar economic asset, is the worth *now* of the benefits of future ownership. In order to calculate brand value one must identify clearly:

(i) the actual benefits of future ownership – that is, the current and future earnings or cash flows of the brand; and

(ii) the multiple or discount rate which needs to be applied to these earnings to take account of inflation and risk.

Interbrand's approach to brand valuation (one which is now widely accepted in many markets around the world) works on the premise that it is brand strength which determines the discount rate, or multiple, to apply to brand earnings. Thus a strong brand provides a high level of confidence that brand earnings will be maintained. High brand strength translates into a low discount rate or a high multiple. Conversely, with a weak brand, one's level of confidence in future earnings is reduced, so the discount rate to be applied to those earnings must be high, or the multiple low.

In our experience this method of valuing brands, focused on brand earnings and a brand's marketing strength, is robust and auditable and provides reliable and realistic values for brands (see Plates 38–43 for examples of brands valued by

209

Interbrand). The success of the model depends of course on the quality of the information put into it – hence it is important to ensure that the requisite marketing, financial and trade mark legal information is brought together in the analysis.

Brand Earnings

A vital factor in determining the value of a brand is its profitability or potential profitability, particularly its profitability over time. However, to arrive at a value it is not enough merely to apply a simple discount rate or multiplier to the post-tax profits of the brand-owning company. First, not all of the profitability of a brand can necessarily be applied to the valuation of that brand. A brand may be essentially a commodity product or may gain much of its profitability from non-brand-related factors. The elements of profitability which do not result from the brand's identity must therefore be excluded. Secondly, the valuation itself may, in the case of an earnings multiple system, be materially affected by using a single, possibly unrepresentative, year's profit. For this reason, a smoothing element should be introduced; generally, a three-year weighted average of historical profits is used. Finally, future projections for the brand are frequently somewhat optimistic so the discounted cash flow model must incorporate a thorough review of expected future performance.

The following issues must therefore be taken into consideration in calculating brand earnings.

Determining brand profits

Since it is the worth of the brand to the business which is being valued it is important that the profit on which this valuation is based is clearly defined. For most purposes this profit should be the fully absorbed profit of the brand after allocation of central overhead costs but before interest charges. Taxation is, of course, also deducted, as will be explained later. For the purposes of evaluating the brand, interest costs are usually ignored since the basis of funding chosen for the brand should not be relevant to the brand's performance.

The elimination of private label production profits

The profits to which a discount factor or an earnings multiple is applied must relate only to the brand being valued and not to other, unbranded goods which may be produced in parallel with the brand but which are not sold under the brand name. These profits may be separately identified by the company through its accounting systems; alternatively, judgement may need to be exercised in assessing the extent of such profits based on production volumes, sales values or other acceptable methods. In so far as 'allocation' is at the heart of much accountancy, the elimination of 'own label' profits is normally entirely feasible.

Remuneration of capital

For the purposes of a valuation, to apply a discount rate or multiple to all the profitability of a brand potentially overvalues that brand. Not all the resulting amount can be attributed to the brand itself – some of it necessarily reflects the value of the other assets employed in the business, such as distribution systems, fixed assets and management. Or, put another way, if one fails to deduct a suitable return for the other assets employed on the brand there will, arguably, be double counting.

Of course, the value of the 'other' assets will vary widely according to the industry concerned. Indeed, it can vary quite widely even within a single industry. Consider, for example, a company marketing two branded soft drinks, Brand X and Brand Y. Brand X is in normal retail distribution and competes with Coca-Cola, Fanta, 7-Up and scores of other brands; Brand Y is sold through distributors who provide a door-to-door delivery service. Both brands may have identical profits yet their brand value will be quite different. Brand Y, for example, may derive little or none of its profits from its brand strength – the profitability of the brand may be exclusively related to its distribution system and the brand itself may play virtually no part in influencing consumer choice. Brand X, on the other hand, may have a powerful consumer franchise and thus be a valuable brand asset.

There are several ways of identifying and eliminating earnings that do not relate to brand strength but the most frequently used system is that of charging the capital tied up in the production of the brand with the return one might expect to achieve if one was simply producing a generic. Assessing this charge obviously requires careful analysis and keen judgment, but as a general rule the non-brand related returns one would expect in an industry where brands play a relatively insignificant rôle (for example, heavy engineering) will be greater than those where brands are critical to success (for example, cosmetics or fragrances). Provided one is dealing with the current cost of assets, a *real* return in the 5–10 per cent range is normal and can be used as a capital remuneration figure.

Taxation

The discount rates or multiples we use are applied to the brand's post-tax profits. A tax rate is normally applied which is the medium-term effective tax rate of the company.

The weighting of historical earnings

For an earnings multiple system, a weighting factor should be applied to historic earnings so as to determine a prudent and conservative level of ongoing profitability to which to apply an appropriate multiple. In many cases a simple weighting of three times the current year, twice the previous year and once the year before is used. These aggregate earnings are then divided by the sum of the weighting factors. However, it may be necessary to review the weighting allocation if forecast future earnings are significantly in excess of the weighted average profit value and are expected to remain at this level in the foreseeable future. It could well be, for example, that historical profits have been depressed by factors now brought under control and it may be appropriate therefore to place greater reliance on more recent earnings when arriving at a valuation.

The restatement of profits to present day values

Since, in the case of an earnings multiple system, historical earnings form the basis of the valuation these values must be re-stated to present day figures by adjustments for inflation. This has the effect of ensuring that performance is reviewed at constant levels. In the case of the discounted cash flow system stripping out of inflation is done as a matter of course as part of the DCF calculation process.

Provision for decline

There is a basic accounting rule that benefits should only be taken when they are earned, but that losses should be provided for as soon as they are foreseen. This rule further implies that, when a brand valuation is done for balance sheet purposes using an earnings multiple approach, future brand profitability must be reviewed so as to see whether the profits on which the valuation is based will be maintained. Where the weighted average historical earnings are clearly below the forecast brand profits in future years, no provision for decline is necessary, provided of course that the forecast is reasonable and can be justified. Where, however, the weighted average earnings are greater than the forecast future brand profits, a provision for decline may be necessary to reflect the reduced level of future profitability.

All these factors must be carefully reviewed when determining brand-related earnings. An example of how these factors are applied is shown in Figure 12.1.

Figure 12.1 Calculating brand earnings

		Year −2	Year −1	Year 0	Year 1	Year 2	Year 3	Year 4	Year 5	Year 6	Year 7	Year 8	Year 9	Year 10
Trading Profit	$000's	750	795	850	925	985	1050	1060	1100	1150	1150	1150	1150	1150
Profits from Own Label Manufacture	$000's	−275	−275	−250	−300	−300	−300	−300	−300	−300	−300	−300	−300	−300
Brand Trading Profit	**$000's**	**475**	**520**	**600**	**625**	**685**	**750**	**760**	**800**	**850**	**850**	**850**	**850**	**850**
Capital Employed	*$000's*	*3500*	*3600*	*3700*	*4000*	*5500*	*5600*	*5600*	*5700*	*5700*	*6000*	*6000*	*6250*	*6250*
Charge for Capital @ 5.0%	$000's	−175	−180	−185	−200	−275	−280	−280	−285	−285	−300	−300	−313	−313
Brand Profit Before Tax	**$000's**	**300**	**340**	**415**	**425**	**410**	**470**	**480**	**515**	**565**	**550**	**550**	**538**	**538**
Tax Payable @ 33.0%	$000's	−99	−112	−137	−140	−135	−155	−158	−170	−186	−182	−182	−177	−177
Brand Earnings	**$000's**	**201**	**228**	**278**	**285**	**275**	**315**	**322**	**345**	**379**	**369**	**369**	**360**	**360**
Inflation		*8.0%*	*5.0%*	*4.0%*	*3.0%*	*3.0%*	*3.0%*	*3.0%*	*3.0%*	*3.0%*	*3.0%*	*3.0%*	*3.0%*	*3.0%*
Brand Earnings Constant Money	**$000's**	**228**	**239**	**278**	**276**	**259**	**288**	**286**	**298**	**317**	**300**	**291**	**276**	**268**

MULTIPLE OF EARNINGS

Brand Earnings	**$000's**	228	239	278
Weightings		1	2	3
Weighted Average	**$000's**	257		
Provision for Decline		0		
Brand Earnings	**$000's**	257		

DISCOUNTED CASH FLOW

		Year 1	Year 2	Year 3	Year 4	Year 5	Year 6	Year 7	Year 8	Year 9	Year 10
Brand Earnings*	**$000's**	276	259	288	286	298	317	300	291	276	268

* This example assumes earnings and cash flow are interchangeable – i.e. capital expenditure equals depreciation.

Brand Strength

The determination of the discount rate, in the case of DCF valuations, or the multiple to be applied to brand profit is derived from an in-depth assessment of brand strength, as it is brand strength which determines the reliability of a brand's future cash flow. An assessment of brand strength requires a detailed review of each brand, its positioning, the market in which it operates, competition, past performance, future plans and risks to the brand. The overall brand strength score is a composite of seven weighted factors, each of which is scored according to clearly established and consistent guidelines. These key factors are as follows:

(i) *Leadership* A brand which leads its market or market sector is generally a more stable and valuable property than a brand lower down the order. To score highly in the area of leadership a brand must be a dominant force in its sector with a strong market share. It must therefore be able strongly to influence its market, set price points, command distribution and resist competitive invasions.

(ii) *Stability* Long-established brands which command consumer loyalty and have become part of the 'fabric' of their markets are particularly valuable and are normally afforded high scores.

(iii) *Market* Brands in markets such as food, drinks and publishing are in most (but not all) cases stronger than brands in, for example, high-tech or high fashion areas as these markets are more vulnerable to technological or taste changes. A brand in a stable but growing market with strong barriers to entry will thus score particularly highly.

(iv) *Geographic Spread* Brands which have strong international acceptance and appeal are inherently stronger than national or regional brands. Significant investment will have been incurred in the geographical development of such brands and they are less susceptible to competitive attack. They are, therefore, more robust and stable assets. Moreover, by no means all brands are capable of crossing cultural and national barriers so those that are must be considered as particularly valuable assets.

(v) *Trend* The overall long-term trend of the brand is an important measure of its ability to remain contemporary and relevant to consumers and hence of its value.

(vi) *Support* Those brands which have received consistent investment and focused support usually have a much stronger franchise than those which have not. While the amount spent in supporting a brand is important the quality of that support is equally significant.

(vii) *Protection* A registered trade mark is a statutory monopoly in a name, device, or in a combination of these two. Other protection may exist at common law, at least in certain countries. The strength and breadth of the brand's protection is critical in assessing its overall strength. Indeed, if the legal basis of the brand is suspect it may not be possible to apply a value to the brand at all.

When assessing brand strength a detailed audit is therefore conducted of each brand. A detailed questionnaire which gives all relevant brand information in a structured and comprehensive way should normally be prepared and completed. Packaging as well as TV and press advertisements will need to be examined and inspection visits carried out to trade and retail outlets. Once a thorough understanding of the brand, its market, competitive factors, trends and so forth has been acquired, the brand is scored on each of the above key factors.

Let us consider how four different brands might be scored.

Brand A This is a leading international toiletries brand operating in a 'mainstream' and stable market sector. The brand has been established for many years and is brand leader or a strong number two in all its major international markets.

Brand B This is a leading food brand which operates in a traditional and stable market but one where tastes are slowly changing with a move away from traditional products and towards convenience foods. The brand has limited export sales and its trade mark protection, though quite strong, is based mainly on common law rather than registered rights.

Brand C This is a secondary but aspiring national soft drinks brand launched just five years ago. The market is dynamic and growing strongly. The brand has been very heavily supported and much has been achieved; it is, however, still early days. Even though export sales are still very small, the brand name, 'get up', and positioning have all been developed with international markets in mind. The brand still has some trade mark registration problems in its home market.

Brand D This is an established but quite small regional brand in a highly fragmented yet stable market.

Based upon detailed brand-by-brand analyses, the scores attributed to each brand might be as follows:

Strength factors	Maximum score	Brand A	Brand B	Brand C	Brand D
Leadership	25	18	19	9	6
Stability	15	11	10	7	11
Market	10	7	6	8	6
Internationality	25	17	5	2	0
Trend	10	6	6	7	5
Support	10	8	7	7	4
Protection	5	5	3	4	3
	100	72	56	44	35

While these scores are hypothetical, they demonstrate the basic 'building blocks' from which an overall brand strength assessment can be derived. This method not only ranks brands in terms of strength, but it also allows brand-by-brand analysis and comparisons and highlights those areas where management could most readily direct its efforts to enhance brand strength and hence brand value. In the case of Brand B, for example, two initiatives immediately present themselves. First, management could consider 'leveraging off' the existing brand strength in a stable but relatively stagnant market to enter sectors of higher growth; secondly, if management were able to exploit the brand in overseas markets, the overall brand strength score would be much improved.

Attributing a Discount Rate or Multiple

The strength of a brand directly determines the reliability of future income flows from that brand so the brand strength analysis can be used to determine the discount rate or the multiple to apply to the brand-related profits; thus the stronger the brand the lower the discount rate or the greater the multiple and *vice versa*. The relationship between brand strength and brand value follows a normal distribution and is represented by a classic 'S' curve such as that shown in Figure 12.2. The shape of the curve is influenced by the following factors:

(i) As a brand's strength increases from virtually zero (an unknown or new brand) to a position as number three or four in a national market the value increases gradually.

(ii) As a brand moves into the number two or number one position in its market and/or becomes known internationally there is an exponential effect on its value.

(iii) Once a brand is established as a powerful world brand its value no longer increases at the same exponential rate even if market share internationally is improved.

But how does one relate the brand's position on the 'S' curve to value? A brand at the bottom point on the curve is easy – a brand with no strength has a multiple of zero or a discount rate of infinity. But what is the multiple or discount rate which should be applied to a notional perfect brand?

Figure 12.2 Brand strength vs. Brand value

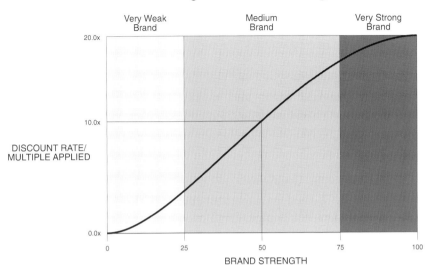

The closest available analogy to the return from a notional perfect brand (that is, one with a brand strength score of 100) is the return from a risk-free investment, although it must be recognised that even the perfect brand does not operate in a risk-free environment. Thus the highest multiple that can be applied will be somewhat lower than that for a risk-free investment and may vary from business to business and industry to industry. Equally, the lowest discount rate which can be used will be higher than the rate of 3–3.5 per cent which is generally applied to a risk-free investment such as a Government bond.

Moreover, other comparable multiples must also be considered, such as those determined by market conditions. The price/earnings (P/E) ratios of industries serving consumer goods markets provide one such indicator of the multiples that can reasonably be considered to apply to brands for balance sheet and similar valuation purposes. Such P/E ratios, however, normally reflect both strong and weak brands as well as commodity and unbranded production. For example, the P/E ratio for the UK food manufacturing sector has varied from 12 to 17 over the last five years.

Therefore the multiple at the high end of the brand strength scale should clearly be greater than the average P/E ratio of the sector in which the company operates and brands at the low end of the brand strength scale should be below this ratio.

Taking into account the risk-free investment analogy, sector P/Es, interest rates and values as determined by actual market conditions in fast-moving-consumer-goods sectors, we have determined that a maximum multiple of 20 for our notional 'perfect' brand is normally appropriate. Brands will be scaled below this multiple according to their brand strength. The discount rates used under the DCF model are inversely linked to the multiple and therefore a minimum rate (that is, for the perfect brand) would be 5 per cent.

The Valuation Calculation

We have seen already how brand earnings are calculated and how brand strength scores are determined for different brands. Figure 12.3 shows how the valuation calculation is determined assuming four different brands with different brand strengths but identical profits. This demonstrates clearly the greater valuation afforded to strong brands, even when brand earnings are identical.

Once the valuation calculation has been performed it is also important to carry out sensitivity analysis on the key underlying assumptions. The major assumptions which should be examined for their impact on the valuation are:

(i)   The multiple applied

(ii)   The tax rate used

(iii)   The capital remuneration rate.

If the valuation is shown to be particularly sensitive to changes in some or all of these assumptions it may be sensible to adopt a particularly prudent approach when valuing the brand. In certain instances, where there is a substantial political or market risk over and above the brand risk, it may

Figure 12.3 Calculating brand value: earnings multiple and DCF methods

		Year −2	Year −1	Year 0	Year 1	Year 2	Year 3	Year 4	Year 5	Year 6	Year 7	Year 8	Year 9	Year 10
Brand Earnings	$000's	201	228	278	285	275	315	322	345	379	369	369	360	360
Inflation		*8.0%*	*5.0%*	*4.0%*	*3.0%*	*3.0%*	*3.0%*	*3.0%*	*3.0%*	*3.0%*	*3.0%*	*3.0%*	*3.0%*	*3.0%*
Brand Earnings Constant Money	$000's	228	239	278	277	259	288	286	298	317	300	291	276	268

MULTIPLE OF EARNINGS BASIS

		Year −2	Year −1	Year 0
Brand Earnings	$000's	228	239	278
Weightings		1	2	3
Weighted Average	$000's			257
Provision for Decline				0
Brand Earnings	$000's			257

Brand Strength Score/Multiple/Value	*Strength*	Multiple	$000's
	72	16.37	4204
	56	11.87	3048
	44	8.13	2088
	35	5.46	1402

DISCOUNTED CASH FLOW BASIS

		Year 0	Year 1	Year 2	Year 3	Year 4	Year 5	Year 6	Year 7	Year 8	Year 9	Year 10
Brand Earnings	$000's		277	259	288	286	298	317	300	291	276	268
Base Discount Rate (Strength Score of 72)			6.11%	6.11%	6.11%	6.11%	6.11%	6.11%	6.11%	6.11%	6.11%	6.11%
Discount Factor		1.000	1.061	1.126	1.195	1.268	1.345	1.427	1.515	1.607	1.705	1.810
Discounted Cash Flow	$000's		261	230	241	226	221	222	198	181	162	148

NPV of Cash Flow to Year 10	$000's	2091
NPV of Cash Flow Beyond Year 10	$000's	2283
Total NPV of Cash Flow	$000's	**4374**

Brand Strength Score/Discount Rate/Value	*Strength*	Multiple	$000's
	72	6.11%	**4373**
	56	8.42%	**3186**
	44	12.30%	**2198**
	35	18.32%	**1492**

also be appropriate to apply an additional discount to the brand value to take account of such special factors.

Portfolio Effect

This methodology does not, of course, take into account the added value which might accrue from the portfolio effect of the brands owned by a company. The reason for this is that the additional financial benefits of the portfolio will already be incorporated in the individual profits of the brands. Nor is it normally appropriate to include an additional weighting for the extra value that a third party might place on the portfolio element since, in most instances, we are assessing the value of a brand to an existing owner.

Other Valuation Applications

This chapter has focused mainly on the technical aspects of brand valuation for balance sheet and related purposes, both 'home grown' and acquired brands. There are, of course, many other situations where brand valuations can usefully be used and where the same basic methodology can be applied. These are discussed in the final chapter of this book and can include mergers and acquisitions, fund-raising, licensing, brand management and brand strategy development. The assessment of the strength of the brand is unlikely to change greatly whatever the purpose of the valuation or evaluation (and this is the area of the valuation process which normally requires the most detailed and time-consuming investigations) though attributable brand earnings and the appropriate multiple could vary considerably. In the case of acquisitions, for example, synergy benefits could be identified and incorporated into the brand profits; also it may be appropriate to include an acquisition premium.

It should also be noted that even when a valuation is based upon notional royalty rates or upon discounted future earnings it is first necessary to identify brand earnings and review carefully the reliability of future income flows. In other words, the key elements of this methodology – the assessment of brand earnings and of brand strength – need to be followed whatever procedure is used to derive a valuation.

Brand valuation will, I believe, play an increasingly important rôle in brand management in the future. Brands which have genuine power in the marketplace are extremely valuable assets and they need to be looked after properly and appropriately for the long term. Brand owners need to understand how the value of these assets can change and to identify which aspects of the brand management mix are important in delivering enhanced value.

BRANDS, CULTURE AND BUSINESS IN JAPAN 13

Keijiro Nakabe
MARUHA CORPORATION

Branding strategy at Taiyo Fishery Co. Limited has always been influenced by changes in Japanese culture and we recently commissioned a complete review of our corporate branding strategy to ensure that we continue to present a corporate image and brand personality that is relevant and appropriate to our various audiences in Japan and elsewhere in the world. The recommendations arising from this review are now being implemented across the group.

The most important of these changes was a decision to change the name and identity of the company itself and, in September 1993, Taiyo Fishery Co. Limited changed its name

Illustration 13.1
The original Taiyo Fishery logo featuring a circle around the hiragana character 'ha' is a graphic representation of the sound of 'Maruha'.

to Maruha Corporation. This is a dramatic step in the company's history, particularly since the company has been in existence for 123 years. The decision to change our corporate name provides powerful evidence of our determination to ensure that, in branding terms, we continue to present the right image.

Illustration 13.2
The new company name and identity was launched in September 1993.

My purpose in this chapter is to explain our approach to branding which in turn may help to shed some light on the importance that Japanese companies attach to brands and branding.

The Importance of Brands in the Japanese Market

I should start off by saying that, in Japan, brands are not seen to be as important a factor as they are in the West. An American businessman is said to have remarked that of all the assets owned by the company the most valuable were the brands – in Japan, even though we believe brands to be an important part of the business mix, such a statement would be unthinkable. Our attitudes towards brands and our views on their rôle in business are utterly different from those espoused in the West.

Western companies often buy and sell their brands. Again, to us in Japan this is unthinkable. To sell one's brands would be seen as an attempt by the parent corporation to prostitute itself in the market place. The company's name and reputation would be seriously damaged by such a move. Furthermore, it would be extremely unlikely for any third party in Japan to be interested in buying the brands of another company – it would besmirch their honour to become involved. To the Western observer this may seem faintly absurd but to the Japanese businessman these issues are of central importance to the way in which business is carried out in Japan.

Our New Corporate Name

The decision to change our corporate name was announced to the press in October 1992. To be honest, we were staggered at the extent of public interest in the name change. Many Japanese corporations changed their name and/or identities during the 1980s and we thought that our particular name change would be seen as just one more example of the same trend. But we were wrong. The depth of feeling and interest provoked by the name change surprised us all.

One reason for the public debate was the familiarity of the Taiyo Fishery logo. This logo, a circle around the hiragana character 'ha', is a graphic representation of the sound 'Maruha'. It has been in use for well over 100 years and is older than the Japanese postal system. A proposed change in the look and style of this logo was therefore bound to cause public debate.

A little background on our company and its history will help to explain how the decision to change this well-established company name and logo came about.

A Short History of Taiyo Fishery

Taiyo Fishery was founded by Ikujiro Nakabe in 1880. The Nakabe family were originally fishermen from Hayashizaki (now in Hyogo Prefecture) who moved to the castle town of Akashi and became fishmongers there under the name of Hayashiya. In those feudal times, merchants in Japan were not allowed to use their surnames, so they used shop names (or brand names) to describe their own stores and the families that worked within them. The Hayashiya name had already been in use for four generations before Ikujiro Nakabe, the company founder, was born. Indeed, the original merchanting name was kept as part of the company name, Hayashikane Shoten, for much of the first half of this century and until the name Taiyo Fishery was adopted as the company name.

Ikujiro Nakabe's first business was that of being a middleman or wholesaler of fresh fish. Ikujiro Nakabe's fleet of small boats would draw up alongside the fishing boats lying offshore, buy their catches on the spot and take the fish to the market for onward sale. Each of the boats in the fleet flew the Maruha flag. Whenever the masters of the fishing boats saw that the Maruha boats were approaching they would start to calculate what sort of price they would be able to command for their catch that day. The Maruha flag became very well known to the Japanese fishing community. In later years Ikujiro also sent his fleet of boats to the Korean

Illustration 13.3
The Maruha flag has been used on the company's fishing fleet for over a hundred years.

fishing grounds so the Korean fishermen also began to recognise the Maruha logo and identity. The international development of the business was thus started at a very early stage.

At first sight, the business of purchasing and distributing fish would seem to be a relatively low-risk high-margin activity. On further examination this is found not to be true. For example, expansion necessitates both the acquisition of boats to carry produce from the fishing boats to the market and the establishment of new sources of produce in other fishing grounds. If fishermen have a good year and there is plenty of business for the middlemen then the cost of this expansion can be funded from ongoing business. But if business is poor then losses can mount up quite quickly. In bad years fishermen also suffer from loss of income and in such times it is the middleman who has the responsibility of ensuring that the fishing community remains in good spirits and has enough food, fuel and subsistence to survive until the next season. The middleman purchased and distributed the catch for the fishermen and also had to absorb the cost of underwriting the welfare of the entire fishing community. The risks involved in the merchanting business were therefore quite considerable.

Ikujiro was unhappy with what he saw to be a business with great downside risk and little upside reward and resolved to become more of a principal than a middleman. Hence he started to build his own fleet of fishing vessels. His timing was impeccable. The creation of the Maruha fishing fleet coincided with the boom years of Japanese fishing in the early part of this century. Very soon Taiyo Fishery had one of the biggest fishing fleets on the Ocean and, until the rules and regulations regarding 200 mile limits became international law, the Maruha flag could be seen on many of the world's great fishing grounds. Maruha vessels fished for all kinds of fish in the Northern Oceans and were equally active in the Southern Oceans looking for whale. The Maruha brand began to be associated not just with the merchanting of fish but also with the catching of fish.

In a further diversification of its operations Taiyo Fishery started to become involved in set-net fishing, whaling and in canning operations too. Over the years, the company built a string of canning, sardine oil and fish meal plants stretching from Korea to Japan.

After the Second World War, the company decided to devote more of its resources to processing foods. By 1955, a decade after the war ended, processed foods accounted for 10 per cent of the company's total sales. Growth in this business has continued right up to the present day.

The Taiyo Fishery business therefore has three strands:

(i)   the original business of purchasing and distributing fish

(ii) the second business of fishing and whaling

(iii) the third and most recent business of manufacturing processed foods

These three businesses have helped to shape perceptions of the Maruha brand identity.

Illustration 13.4

The new corporate brand, Maruha, is used to endorse the company's processed foods products – the brand stands for stability, trust and reliability.

The Rôle of Brands in the Fishing Industry

The principal business in which the company has been involved, namely purchasing and distributing fish, is the one business where brands have a very limited rôle. The middleman in the fish business is dealing in a commodity, fish, and the need for branding is not very acute. We realised that if we were going to add any value at all to the middleman rôle, we would have to understand what branding could offer and restructure our business to benefit as much as possible from branding techniques but within the limitations of our own particular market. In a sense therefore we had to work even harder than many branded goods companies in order to obtain the benefits from good branding.

Throughout our history we have always fought fiercely to gain a competitive advantage and then to protect the rights in that advantage – for example, through the protection afforded by trade marks and brands. As long ago as 1957 we noted that fish was being packed in trays and labelled in the US market under brand names. We brought the concept of branding fish to the Japanese market. Within a year we were exporting frozen rainbow trout from the north east of Japan back to Los Angeles under the 'Stream Fresh' label. This was the first time that a Japanese company actually marketed fish under a brand name, albeit a highly descriptive one.

The brand name operates as an indicator of quality and freshness. Consumers look for brands because they provide consumers with important messages of reassurance and confidence. Branding in the fish market is now common-place – supermarket freezers and display cabinets are crammed full of different brands of fish. We use our brands to create a strong link of trust and reassurance with our customers.

The importance of brands and branding in the fish market has made us aware of the potential power and value of strong and well-managed brands. In recognition of this we have made many internal changes and reforms to ensure that our brands continue to be strong and powerful. This emphasis on the importance of brands was the main driving force behind our decision to change the corporate name and identity to make it reflect more accurately the reality of the company's offer.

The MMBM Programme

One of the most important strategic initiatives in the branding field in recent years was the development of what we call the MMBM Programme (which translates to 'Maruha Power Brand Marketing Programme' in English), first announced in February 1993. The decision to change our corporate name was tied up very closely with the MMBM Programme and it is therefore worth exploring in more detail.

The MMBM Programme addresses the needs of all our individual brands in their respective product areas but also ensures that our portfolio of brands as a whole helps to build and reinforce the strength and power of the overall corporate brand image.

We have, we believe, four major brands with distinctive brand positionings and personalities. Each of these brands acts as a communicator of the strengths and qualities of the underlying businesses. They present our operations in a distinctive and attractive manner and provide our employees with a focal rallying point. Each brand may be separate but they all serve to enhance the reputation and prestige of the parent corporate brand.

The basic philosophy behind the MMBM Programme is to achieve growth and profitability for the group as a whole through well-organised branding of each of the constituent parts. Some individual activities may appear on the surface to be unprofitable but further analysis will reveal that they are part of a strategy designed to enhance the image and appeal of the whole. When Honda went into Formula 1 racing it knew that it was going to invest a large amount of money in what is one of the world's most expensive sports. But it went ahead with the investment because it could see that the spin-offs for their car sales business would be considerable. If

Honda has good enough technology to win Formula 1 races then it must have sufficiently good technology to manufacture saloon and sports cars for the general public.

The whole basis of promotional activity is to encourage consumers to try out something which will not cost them very much and then to impress them so much with the quality of that experience that they come back for more. Supermarkets run price promotions with the express purpose of attracting customers into the store. Once in the store it is hoped that consumers will buy more than just those products being promoted.

The marketing programme, be it Formula 1 racing for Honda or a cheap price promotion for a supermarket, is designed to enhance awareness of the brand and to encourage consumer purchase. The MMBM Programme works in exactly the same way.

The MMBM Programme has identified four brands each of which have a strategic marketing rôle for the group.

The power brand – Maruha

In Figure 13.1 it can be seen that the main brand is Maruha. Maruha is the power brand of the company. The products

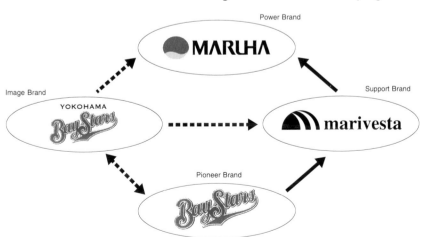

Figure 13.1 The MMBM programme

endorsed by the Maruha brand name are in the processed foods field – this now represents the largest proportion of overall group sales and profits. The Maruha brand is our flagship brand and must be managed with great skill. We cannot afford anything to go wrong with the Maruha brand – it must continue to stand for stability, trust and reliability. The products and services promoted under the Maruha name are not expected to show spectacular growth but sales forecasts anticipate that growth will be the same as that of the market as a whole. The Maruha brand is the cornerstone of the group.

The support brand – Marivesta

The support brand is Marivesta, a brand of fish. Much of our current turnover is accounted for by our original business of trading as middlemen in fish. Importing fish from around the world and ensuring that it arrives in Japan at the peak of freshness and taste is no easy task. We have developed highly specialised skills in the purchasing, transportation and distribution of fish from fishing grounds all around the world. Our buyers ensure that we purchase produce of the right quality, freshness and flavour at the best prices available in the market. Our transportation and distribution teams ensure that when the fish is served to customers back in Japan it has lost none of its freshness and flavour. Much of the fish imported to Japan is served to customers uncooked – consequently the quality and taste of the fish must be perfect.

The brand Marivesta has come to represent the very best in quality, freshness and taste. Marivesta fish contributes to a richer dining experience for customers all over Japan. The prestige and scale of our fish trading operation is such that we can envisage it becoming the main brand of the group in the future, taking over from Maruha.

A support brand has two rôles in the MMBM Programme. First it must support the power brand and act as a complement to it. But secondly, and as importantly, it must continue to challenge the power brand with a view, ultimately, to replacing it. This rivalry between brands is

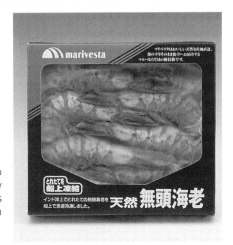

Illustration 13.5
Marivesta is a support brand used to endorse the Taiyo Fishery's many and varied fish products – it has come to represent the very best in quality, freshness and taste.

well known in other companies (Procter & Gamble and Unilever provide two very good examples of Western organisations where brands are encouraged to compete with each other) and serves to promote energy and dynamism into the brand management function.

The image brand – Yokohama BayStars

An image brand serves to promote the image and reputation of the whole group – it captures the group's personality in an exciting and dynamic manner and can be 'borrowed' by the other brands as and when required. We referred above to the Honda brand in Formula 1 racing which is clearly operating as an image brand generating strong awareness for the brand around the world. For our group the image brand is the Yokohama BayStars, one of Japan's leading baseball teams. The success and publicity given to this baseball team generates enormous awareness for Maruha's other brands. The story of the Yokohama BayStars is set out separately below.

The pioneer brand – BayStars

A pioneer brand has the objective, as its name suggests, of developing new products and services in fields outside the

Illustration 13.6

The Yokohama BayStars is the image brand for the Maruha group. The success and publicity given to the BayStars generates enormous awareness for Maruha's other brands.

core businesses of the group. The target markets for these new products and services are outside the core areas served by the group's power and support brands and therefore a separate name and identity is required. The BayStars name is used to fulfil this rôle. The brand is experimental, new, modern, pioneering, challenging and forward-looking – it is the incubator for all of our future products and services.

We see a wide range of products and services falling neatly under the BayStars umbrella brand:

(i)   Sports or sports-related products

(ii) New food products recognised as being new to the market

(iii) Food products from around the world refined and adapted to suit the tastes of the Japanese market

(iv) Specially priced personal use products

(v)   Products that are associated strongly with Yokohama's heritage and history.

In due course the pioneer brand may become a support brand and in the long term may challenge for the ultimate position of power brand.

As can be seen from the above, the MMBM Programme defines different rôles and functions for each of the main brands within the group. Each brand has its own positioning and brand personality and is encouraged to pursue its own strategic direction. The contrast between each of the main brands in our company creates an exciting and dynamic environment for the group. We have found that this structure has created a highly motivational environment for management and staff.

The MMBM Programme was developed primarily to change internal attitudes and to encourage people to think more proactively about how brands and branding could assist the company in achieving its goals and ambitions. One aspect of the MMBM Programme that has had a major impact externally as well as internally has been the development of the new name and identity for our baseball team.

The Yokohama BayStars

The announcement of the new name and identity for the Yokohama BayStars was one of the biggest stories of the sporting year. It created a new era in baseball in Japan for the Yokohama BayStars is now the only team in baseball to have a brand name which has no relationship to the sponsoring company. So, just as we pioneered the branding of fish in this country, so too we are pioneering the branding and marketing of baseball.

Baseball is Japan's most popular game. The traditions and customs associated with the sport are part of the fabric of life in Japan just as they are in the USA. Baseball has been played in Japan for more than 100 years and Taiyo has owned its own team since 1950, shortly after the professional game got off the ground in Japan. The team was named the Taiyo Whales and had its first major success in winning the League Championship in 1960. The team has a powerful following in the Yokohama area and is well supported by its fans at all games.

While the internal review on the importance of brands and branding was being undertaken by the company we were

Illustration 13.7
The Yokohama BayStars is the first Japanese team to be linked in branding terms to the community it serves rather than the corporation which sponsors it – this approach has been well received by the public.

keen to test the relevance and appropriateness of the Taiyo Whales name. We wanted to review the strength of all of our brands and not just of the operational brands.

Some time ago it occurred to me that it might no longer be appropriate to have our corporate name so strongly linked to that of our baseball team. The link between baseball teams and corporate sponsors has historically been very close in Japan and, without this sponsorship, many teams would surely fail. Japanese companies accept the losses involved in sponsorship because they receive highly attractive spin-off benefits in terms of public relations, advertising, image-building, and so on. But recent developments in Japan's fastest growing new sport, soccer, have changed my own views on the most appropriate way to go forward with team sponsorship in baseball.

The J League, Japan's first professional soccer league, was launched in 1993 and will test an entirely new concept in Japanese sport – namely, that teams should have a close connection with the communities they serve rather than with their sponsoring companies. Hence soccer is the complete antithesis to baseball in branding terms. Soccer is intent upon becoming closer to the general public whereas baseball is still oriented very heavily towards the corporate world. It is my view that this switch in the emphasis of sports sponsorship from corporate orientation to public orientation is symptomatic of deep-rooted changes taking place in Japanese society as a whole. It is of course too early to assess whether or not the soccer experiment is going to be a success but I believe that the underlying trend is in the right direction.

As part of the naming review for the Taiyo Whales we decided to explore naming alternatives that were focused more upon the community served by the baseball team rather than on the team's ownership. The name Yokohama BayStars was eventually adopted. It was felt that this name refocused the team on the local community but also created a new opportunity to develop a powerful brand out of the BayStars name.

The public reaction to the new team name has been beyond our wildest expectations. The local community have taken the name to their hearts – the fans are even more passionate in their support for the team than they have ever been. The low-key corporate sponsorship has also worked to our benefit: the fans know that the team is sponsored by Taiyo Fishery as main sponsor but delight in it having a separate brand name and identity. Unlike other teams in the League, the Yokohama BayStars uniform livery has no corporate logo or other identifying device to link the team with Taiyo.

The Future

As Japanese business managers we must turn our attention increasingly to the opportunities that exist in the global market place. Borders are becoming less and less of a hindrance and it is just a matter of time before free trade becomes a reality. We must consider what effect these macro-economic developments will have on the way in which we manage our brands in our various markets around the world.

In my view every company must ensure that all its brands are sufficiently strong to stand on their own feet. If they are not it must be questionable why they exist. It is our goal to ensure that our four main brands, Maruha, Marivesta, BayStars and Yokohama BayStars, are able to develop independently as strong brands yet within the framework of a group strategy. We are devoted to building our brands and to enhancing their strength and we believe that an increasing number of Japanese corporations will adopt a similar philosophy.

Japanese business will also no doubt be increasingly influenced by Western influences and in particular the new marketing and branding techniques being developed in the West. Japanese companies must be prepared to listen to what is happening in the West and apply these practices in the Japanese market.

Maruha Corporation is well placed to benefit from the opportunities that face us as we start the next stage in the evolution of our company. With our focus on the continuing enhancement of our brand power we believe we have the right strategy with which to succeed.

BRAND POWER: THE FUTURE 14

John Murphy
Chairman
INTERBRAND GROUP PLC

The reasons for the rapid growth of interest in brands are several. First, it came to be more generally recognised (though, it should be said, in a rather imperfect and ill-formed way) that certain businesses, which were not especially rich in tangible assets, were performing consistently and powerfully and seemed able to produce superior cash flows to, arguably, more 'conventional' companies. Such companies included businesses such as Apple Computer, Coca-Cola, Guinness and Unilever. Second, analysts and investors started to recognise that such businesses had an added, hidden dimension which set them apart from many others and which seemed to enable them to produce higher quality earnings. At this stage it was not widely recognised that the intangible factor present in such companies was 'intellectual property', mainly brands but also patents, copyrights and designs; nor was it widely recognised that 'intellectual property' (the term used by lawyers to describe such intangibles) or 'intangible assets' (the term used by accountants to describe the self-same assets) are a very specific type of asset which, in many respects, resemble tangible assets.

Trade marks (the specific intellectual property rights which are at the heart of brands), patents, copyrights and designs are crisp pieces of property in which their owners can enjoy specific title; they are not therefore amorphous, generalised properties where title or ownership may be questionable. But

241

the rights residing in brands are different from most other intellectual property rights in one important respect – whereas patents, copyrights and designs have a finite life and then expire, becoming available to all-comers, trade mark rights can continue indefinitely, becoming stronger and more valuable all the time, provided they are properly used and looked after.

So even though a generalised predisposition existed by the 1980s to 'honour' certain types of companies, the distinguishing feature which set such companies apart from others was not clearly recognised. But, in the second half of the 1980s this situation changed, due almost entirely to a succession of major acquisitions of branded goods businesses, mainly in the foods and drinks sector. In the 1980s a scramble developed on the part of companies such as Philip Morris, Nestlé, BSN, Grand Metropolitan and Guinness for the control of leading international branded goods businesses and, as a result, the value and power of brands came to be recognised in an altogether more specific fashion.

Developing new brands from scratch is a highly risky and exceptionally expensive business and this, combined with the relative rarity of strong international brands, ensured that brands such as Smirnoff and Kraft commanded high prices. At first, analysts attributed the wish by predators to acquire brand-rich companies to 'industry rationalisation' and 'economies of scale', factors which arguably could be applied equally to steel-producing companies or shipbuilders but, particularly following a Herculean battle between the Swiss giants Nestlé and Jacobs-Suchard for control of Britain's Rowntree company, a more specific rationale was advanced for this merger and acquisition activity – a battle was taking place for the control of international brands.

During the 1988 battle for control of Rowntree, the management of that company developed, as an integral plank of its defence, the argument that the company's brands were so powerful and valuable that the various bids should be rejected out-of-hand as they should be considered insufficient to command control of such valuable brands. At the same time, local politicians and trades union officials from Rowntree's home city of York introduced into the battle a note of brand nationalism: they argued that Rowntree's brands somehow were national treasures and should not fall into the hands of the predatory Swiss, an argument which the Mayor of York took to Nestlé's Head Office in Vevey, Switzerland, a confrontation which appeared on the BBC's National TV News.

In the event, the spirited bid defence coupled with the rivalry which existed between Nestlé and Jacobs-Suchard and which manifested itself during the takeover bid, ensured that a full price was gained for Rowntree – it was sold eventually for some £2.5 billion, two and a half times the pre-bid price and eight times the tangible net asset valuation.

The effect of this bid on the recognition of brand values and brand power was electrifying, at least in Britain and the rest of Europe. A systematic re-rating took place of brand-rich companies by stock markets and the word 'brand', formerly in common use only by marketing people, entered the vocabulary of accountants, analysts, financial journalists, bankers and general managers.

Brands on the Balance Sheet

But the 1980s mergers and acquisitions activity had, too, a number of knock-on effects, particularly in the area of accountancy. For generations accountants have been altogether more comfortable when accounting for things they can touch than things they cannot, like intangibles. At a time when the *worth* of a business was largely the sum of its tangible assets this did not present great difficulties. But the growing importance of intangible assets placed a great strain on old certainties. Most of the 'value' being acquired by the predators of branded goods businesses such as Rowntree was by definition intangible in nature – branded goods companies do not generally have enormous tangible asset bases – so tangible assets frequently represented only a minor part of such transactions. (See Figure 14.1).

Conventionally, all parts of an acquisition other than the tangible elements are lumped together by accountants under the non-discriminating term 'goodwill'. This generalised term

Figure 14.1 Brands purchased 1988/90 — goodwill as a percentage of purchase price

Vendor	Acquirer	Goodwill (%)
Rowntree	Nestlé	83
Pillsbury	Grand Metropolitan	85
Trebor	Cadbury-Schweppes	75
Verkade	United Biscuits	66

can therefore embrace, at one end of the scale, trade marks, patents, copyrights and licensing agreements, all relatively 'crisp' assets and, at the other end of the scale, altogether more amorphous, perhaps even transitory assets such as the management team and relationships with customers. But, in addition, the 'goodwill' item in an acquisition often includes a premium paid to gain control, a premium which, in certain instances, may be shown to be far from prudent; thus part of the goodwill figure may represent no underlying assets at all, tangible or intangible.

Despite the fact that the various elements swept together under the term 'goodwill' vary widely in their nature, 'tangibility' and potency, accountants have, historically, insisted that they all be lumped together in their accounting treatment. Thus in Britain and Australasia it has been normal to write off against reserves the goodwill element of an acquisition while tangible assets, on the other hand, which are frequently of only limited interest to the acquiring company and may well be quickly rationalised, are considered sufficiently worthy to be transferred straight to the acquiring company's balance sheet. (Amortisation of goodwill through the profit and loss account is also permitted in the UK but, because this has an obvious and immediate impact on earnings per share, has seldom been a preferred option.) But, in the USA and parts of Europe accountancy regulations have not permitted a write-off of goodwill against reserves but have insisted instead that goodwill is taken on to the balance sheet and then expunged from it by amortisation through the profit and loss account over a period of years, a procedure which can have a severely adverse effect both on profits and earnings per share.

These differing accounting treatments of the huge goodwill element necessarily arising on the acquisition of branded goods businesses had a number of effects. In the USA, for example, merger and acquisition ardour in the branded goods area was severely damped down by the amortisation of goodwill provisions, though not in the case of foreign predators such as Britain's Grand Metropolitan, now the owners of Pillsbury, and Australia's News Corporation, now the owners of Twentieth-Century Fox Corporation, as such companies were not constrained in their home countries by US accounting regulations.

None the less, some US companies, especially Philip Morris, had such massively strong cash flows as not to be concerned overmuch about the dilutive effect on profits of goodwill amortisation and remained active acquirors of branded goods businesses such as Kraft (see Plate 44). Also, highly-leveraged buy-out specialists such as Kohlberg Kravis Roberts, the firm which acquired RJR Nabisco in a bitter takeover battle, were also relatively unconcerned about the dilutive effect of goodwill amortisation on profits as their structure was, essentially, 'artificial' and cash flow is more important to the success of a leveraged buy-out than disclosed profit due to the high level of debt servicing.

Generally, however, differing accounting treatments of goodwill resulted in relatively low interest in the acquisition of branded goods businesses by US companies but intense activity, on the other hand, by British and some other companies who were able to write-off acquired goodwill against reserves without adversely affecting profits. But whilst American companies cried 'foul' and accused their overseas competitors of taking advantage of a less than level playing field, those same overseas competitors were starting to find that the erosion of reserves by goodwill write-offs was not a procedure entirely without problems.

It is important for companies to maintain strong balance sheets not just for reasons of corporate pride but also because balance sheet tests are used by, for example, providers of finance to calculate gearing, and by Stock Exchanges when setting class tests. (Class tests determine those decisions which can be left to Board approval and those which require the approval of all shareholders.)

But the main reason why companies deeply resented the erosion of their balance sheets through goodwill write-offs was that they disliked the intangible element of an acquisition being treated as a form of 'fool's gold' which somehow has to be conveniently got rid of as quickly as possible. They knew that much of 'goodwill' constituted very good assets indeed – brands – to which they had clear title and which were eminently transferable, should they so wish.

Companies such as Nestlé, Grand Metropolitan, Philip Morris, BSN, Guinness, Cadbury–Schweppes and United Biscuits are not fools. They do not pay huge sums for branded goods businesses with relatively modest tangible assets on a whim or because it is fashionable to do so or because they get caught up in a form of bid fever. They do so because they recognise that such companies possess specific assets – brands – which are potent, valuable and rare. Yet accountancy has, historically, been unable to accommodate these assets. The plant and machinery on which the branded goods are produced, and which may in fact be of relatively little interest to the acquiring company, can be readily accommodated in the new, enlarged balance sheet but the brands themselves, the assets which drove the deal in the first place, have somehow to be driven off the balance sheet.

In 1988 Grand Metropolitan decided to take pre-emptive action to correct this accounting anomaly and included a valuation of the recently acquired brand Smirnoff, along with certain other acquired brands, on its balance sheet at a sum of £608 million (over $1 billion). Grand Met's initiative was soon taken up by Ranks Hovis McDougall, the major British food company, who added all its brands to its balance sheet whether acquired or otherwise, as well as by firms such as United Biscuits, Guinness and Cadbury–Schweppes.

The resultant 'brands on the balance sheet' debate has caused a furore and has thrown the accounting profession in the UK and elsewhere into much confusion. Concerns have been expressed about the methodologies used to value brands (though brand valuers would retort that these are at least as reliable as the approaches used for generations to value other dedicated economic assets) and the 'brands on the balance sheet' debate has also widened into a much wider debate about the nature of the balance sheet (is it merely a statement of unexpensed costs or should it purport to reflect underlying worth and strength?) and the way in which accountants should account in the modern world.

The issues involved are complex ones and are not capable of easy solution – without doubt accounting for intangibles is altogether more complex than accounting purely for tangibles. Moreover, national accounting regulatory bodies such as the UK's Accounting Standards Board have to pay close attention to the requirements of the International Accounting Standards Committee, a body which is struggling valiantly against seemingly overwhelming odds to standardise accounting on a worldwide basis.

Brand Evaluation

But accounting for brands on the balance sheet is merely a technical exercise – whether or not accountants include brands on balance sheets they still have great potency and value and therefore will attract the attention of managers, investors, bankers, analysts and others. Therefore, even though it was in large part the balance sheet debate which stimulated the current high level of interest in brands this interest will, we are sure, be sustained as will the need to measure and evaluate these assets. Moreover, the meticulous, analytical evaluation techniques developed for balance sheet purposes and designed to be sufficiently robust to permit the accounts to receive a clean audit certificate have proved to be extremely useful for a host of other brand-related applications stimulated by the increased interest in brands. These include:

Mergers & Acquisitions Given that much or most of the value of target businesses may be represented by brands, clearly it is of critical importance for an acquiror, whether hostile or not, as well as for a vendor to understand and evaluate those brands in detail including their worth, their stability and their extension capability.

Disposals The current focus on brands has led many companies to recognise that they cannot support properly all their brands or that certain brands could be worth more to a third party than to their current owners. Brand evaluation techniques can be used to judge which brands to dispose of and their possible worth to a third party.

Licensing Brand licensing, either to third-parties or internally (the latter, frequently, for reasons of tax planning – after all, one would not allow an outsider to use one's brands for free so why not make one's own subsidiaries pay for the use of corporate property?) is an increasingly common practice much assisted by formal brand valuations.

Investor Relations Brands provide their owners with stability and a much enhanced quality of earnings, as companies such as Sara Lee, Coca-Cola, Procter & Gamble and Unilever have shown conclusively in the recent recession. Clearly, if companies own strong and valuable brand assets they should demonstrate this to analysts and investors even if they do not include brands on their balance sheets.

Fund Raising Brands frequently represent robust assets against which to seek or provide funds. In our experience brand valuations are playing an increasingly prominent rôle in the area of fund raising.

Strategy Development But, most importantly, companies are applying brand evaluation techniques in order to understand and manage their brands better. Brand evaluation involves a detailed examination of a brand from a marketing, a financial and a legal perspective; it also examines the brand's performance, prospects, market opportunities and competition. It thus provides a superb tool for strategy development, either on a portfolio or on a brand-by-brand basis.

The brands on the balance sheet debate has, therefore, been instrumental in forcing investors, analysts, accountants and, indeed, management to focus on those assets which *really* constitute the true 'worth' of many businesses and which are therefore critical to corporate success.

The Future

Fuelled by intense merger and acquisition activity and, as a result, by heightened interest from accountants, investors, analysts and bankers, brands and branding reached a level of interest at the end of the 1980s which would have been unthinkable only a few years earlier. But will this new interest in brands be sustained? Will brands continue to grow in importance? And if so, what are the challenges facing those of us involved with brands and branding?

Modern, sophisticated branding is now concerned increasingly with a brand's *gestalt*, with assembling and maintaining in a brand a mix of values, both tangible and intangible, which are relevant to consumers and which meaningfully and appropriately distinguish one supplier's brand from that of another. The art of successful branding lies in selecting and blending these elements so that the result is perceived by consumers to be uniquely attractive and influential on the purchasing decision.

Over the years branded products have consistently succeeded over unbranded products. Coca-Cola (Plate 45), first marketed in the 1880s, succeeded because it offered consumers consistent, reliable quality at a fair price and soon the unbranded colas and soft drinks served by every drug store in the USA had to give way to the power of the brand. In the area of prepared meals the McDonald's brand (Plate 46) had the same effect. Prior to the rise of McDonald's every town in America had its diners and restaurants yet quality was inconsistent and value variable. McDonald's, through its unique franchising and quality control system, was able to 'brand' its prepared meals and has thrived at the expense of its unbranded competitors.

Branded products and services have now invaded almost every area of business – foods, drinks, cosmetics, automotive, even hospital services and drain clearance. In time, no doubt, as entrepreneurs figure out a way to offer consistent, branded products and services in areas such as fresh meat, vegetables, house cleaning, newspaper delivery and window cleaning, these products and services will become branded too.

We have no doubt, therefore, that the concept of branding will remain increasingly relevant well into the twenty-first Century. But how will it develop?

Managing and Exploiting Brands

The brand management function in many companies has traditionally been a training ground for high flyers whose main task has been that of maintaining a link between the company and its advertising and sales promotion agencies. The increased focus on, and interest in, brands seems certain to lead to a fundamental reappraisal of the rôle and status of brand management. Brand managers will be required to take a much more entrepreneurial view of their brands and will be held accountable for their profitability and for a proper return on brand assets, tangible and intangible. Several major companies are already redefining the marketing function and overhauling the brand management system. Recently one major brand owner, when appointing a new director to the board, specifically recognised this by changing the title from Director of Marketing to Director of Brands.

But a redefinition of the rôle of brand management and the elevation of brand management's status is only a first step – brand managers also require much more incisive tools to assist them in the better management of these most rare and valuable assets.

Companies such as Unilever, Coca-Cola and Mars have come, over the years, to recognise that brand management is still very much an art and not a science and that brands should be managed conservatively with more important brand-related decisions taken at a relatively senior level in the company. They also search constantly for new, improved tools to help with the decision-making process.

In most companies brand management receives on a regular basis a mass of market share data which is supplemented periodically with qualitative research but, overall, the brand-related information which is available to management is extremely fragmentary in nature. In practice, therefore, many managers come to make profound decisions about their brands largely on the basis of hunch or anecdote or on the basis of a single piece of data – for example, an awareness study. However, these pieces of information often provide less than a full picture and managers have even in some instances made idiosyncratic decisions about which information they cared to act upon and which they chose to ignore.

The recent tendency to treat brands as specific assets each with its own personality, appeals, cash flows and development potential has led companies to begin viewing their brand assets in an altogether more 'holistic' way. Brand evaluation models have been developed which provide the means to carry out detailed investigative analyses of brands and which therefore give brand management a clearer 'overview' of a brand and of its strengths and weaknesses, development potential and prospects for growth. These brand evaluation models allow those charged with the task of brand management to formulate and test appropriate strategies for their brands.

Such models assess and track in an objective, comparable fashion the key elements of brand strength (for example, the brand's position in its sector; its consumer appeal; the market in which the brand operates; the brand's internationality, or otherwise; the support given to the brand; its performance *versus* competition, and so on) as well as the brand's financial performance. As the *strength* of a brand is a direct measure of the *reliability* of that brand's future earnings, brand strength can be used to set a multiple to apply to actual brand earnings or a discount rate to apply to forecast brand earnings. The brand strength, combined with brand earnings, provides therefore a means of deriving a brand value. Moreover, each step of the evaluation process provides management with useful data and with a flexible and incisive analytical tool which can be used to improve the performance of brands and brand management. The evaluation process ensures too that a proper overview is taken of the brand and of the entire portfolio so that management is not thrown off course by the latest piece of data which comes to light.

The Corporate Brand

While it is tempting to regard branding as being solely the preserve of packaged goods businesses, an important trend in the branding area is towards a much greater recognition of the importance and power of the corporate brand by businesses who, only a few years ago, might not even have considered that they owned a brand. Thus industrial corporations, insurance companies and enterprises involved in the business-to-business sector have all come to recognise that their corporate brand and the way in which it is perceived by its various key audiences – shareholders, analysts, suppliers staff, customers, and so on – can be critical to business success.

In many instances, the start of a specific interest in the corporate brand is marked by an overhaul of the firm's corporate identity but, increasingly, firms are recognising that this may only be the first step in a long process designed to ensure that an attractive, appropriate and differentiated corporate personality is presented to the world and that this personality pervades the entire organisation.

We are also finding that firms such as Nestlé, Mars and Unilever, who have in the past focused largely on individual brands without any large measure of corporate branding, are finding the costs of individual brand support so high that the endorsed approach – use of both a product brand *and* a corporate brand – is becoming increasingly attractive and necessary.

The International Scene

The trends in branding which we have described are most noticeable in Western Europe, North America and Austra-lasia but they are by no means confined to these areas. Japan for example which, hitherto, has dominated mainly in automotive, industrial and consumer durables sectors, is increasingly seeking to establish international power brands in areas such as financial services, toiletries and food and drink as is evidenced by the activities of companies such as Nomura, Kao, Shiseido, Ajinomoto and Suntory.

Turning to Eastern Europe, we can also anticipate that, after an early assault on Eastern European markets by Western brands, indigenous brands will gradually fight back and some will come to establish themselves outside their home markets. Indeed, even though there is a powerful trend towards the globalisation of branding with international power brands such as Heineken (Plate 47), Benetton and Swatch (Plate 48) consolidating their positions on a world basis, the constant broadening of consumer tastes means that opportunities constantly arise for innovative, differentiated brands, most of which start life as niche brands in local markets.

The apparent paradox of an increasing globalisation of brands coupled with the concurrent growth of differentiated, niche brands is caused by two opposing influences. On the one hand, international brands take advantage of market overlaps, cross-border advertising, increased travel and the benefits afforded by increased scale; they also afford to major companies a coherence and focus to their international affairs which would be impossible with a proliferation of more focused local brands. But, on the other hand, local brands can be closely adapted to particular needs, take advantage of niche opportunities and can be flexible and highly adaptable. We therefore see these two apparently contradictory tendencies continuing to operate together and we anticipate, as a result, a constant enrichment of the branding landscape.

The Rôle of Advertising Agencies

For at least three decades after the Second World War brand owners routinely turned to their advertising agencies for much of their required branding and marketing advice.

Indeed, agencies were often seen as the custodians of a company's brands and the major influence on brand development policies.

However, as brands have come increasingly to be viewed as both valuable and important, companies have become reluctant to hand over management responsibility for them to third parties. Agencies, as a result, have found that their 'custodial' rôle has diminished and that the services they are required to provide are increasingly focused on the design and production of advertisements and the purchasing of media rather than on strategic brand management advice. The implications for agencies are profound and this adjustment of rôles, coupled with downward pressure on agency commissions, has led to major structural changes in the industry.

But it is not just agencies who are being forced to change – as companies pay more attention to their brands they are also demanding better market research data, a more focused, strategic approach to product and packaging design and even, in some cases, new financial systems which are brand-centric rather than product, or production, -centric. The growth of brand power is therefore having a knock-on effect throughout the marketing services industry, one which is benefiting many companies but causing serious problems for others.

Conclusions

The Chairman of one of the world's largest brewers remarked recently that once he started to see his company as, in effect, a portfolio of brands and not as a huge brewing enterprise producing different grades and types of beer, he acquired an entirely new vision of his business and of its performance and prospects. He was then able to communicate this vision to investors and analysts as well as to management and staff, a process which resulted in a series of initiatives, internally and through acquisition, which have transformed the company.

Though a focus on brands may not in all cases yield such dramatic results, I believe that the development and exploitation of brands – be they product brands, service brands or corporate brands – will continue to offer significant rewards and, indeed, that brands and branding will become increasingly important as developed countries move to a more sophisticated 'added value' type of economy. But, at the same time, we need to learn better how to manage, exploit and develop brand assets. At present our knowledge of how best to manage brands is often rudimentary; better brand management would clearly yield enormous rewards.